MW00989133

Praise for *Sabbaticals*

"In an age of what seems like unprecedented cases of pastoral fatigue and burnout, Rusty provides a timely and Biblical defense for the necessity of sabbatical rest. Pastors and elders need to read and take heed!"

> **Ronnie Martin**, Lead Pastor of Substance Church and
> co-author of *The Bridezilla of Christ*

"A sabbatical is a gift — one that many people will never experience in their lives. If you receive this gift, you have a responsibility to steward it well. As one who has wasted a sabbatical in the past by over-scheduling myself, I know well how much this book is needed. And, even though I'm years away from my next sabbatical, I'm already planning how I will use this book to steward that one well."

> **Timothy Paul Jones**, Ph.D., Associate Vice President at
> The Southern Baptist Theological Seminary and
> elder at Sojourn Community Church Midtown

"This book may save your life. It certainly will save your ministry, and possibly even more. Pastor Rusty McKie writes with candor, clarity, and experience on a pivotal issue rarely pursued in the modern church. Order copies for each pastor on your team, discuss and make a plan. When that's over, take a nap . . . for the glory of God."

> **Charlie Swain**, Lead Pastor, The Church at Cane Bay,
> Summerville, SC

"Rusty has masterfully and appropriately made a clear biblical case for sabbaticals. As an older pastor who viewed sabbaticals as a creative construct of tired and worn-out Millennials, *Sabbaticals* caused me to rethink my viewpoint. His Philosophy section — a theology of work and rest, captivated my interest. The book is so well conceived and written that it was a joy to read from cover to cover. Rusty has set the new "gold standard" as *Sabbaticals* is the best comprehensive work of its kind on this highly misunderstood ministry issue."

Tim Beltz, Pastor, Author, Church Consultant, and
former Executive Pastor

"As a pastor's wife and someone who consistently (and stubbornly) butts up against my own limits, I'm so grateful for Rusty McKie's new book, *Sabbaticals*. Of all people, pastors might just be the last people willing to take a break. But of all people, pastors also have a unique opportunity to model humility and dependence in front of their congregations by learning to rest well. With care and careful teaching, McKie offers churches and pastors the practical wisdom they need to understand and implement sabbatical practice."

Hannah Anderson, Author of *Humble Roots: How
Humility Grounds and Nourishes Your Soul*

"One of the lesser-considered places where God reveals his heart to us is in his law — specifically the law of Sabbath. Have we ever stopped to marvel at how God loves us so much that he commands our rest? The God of Scripture, in contrast to the world's anxiety system, declares 'well done' before we do any work at all. The last words of Jesus' life, 'It is finished,' have now become the first words for ours. These gospel realities beckon us back to the old and life-giving way of revering rest as much as work, leisure as much as productivity, being still as much as being busy. In this short but important volume, Rusty provides a roadmap for living Sabbath well. Not only do I recommend it, I also need it personally."

Scott Sauls, Senior Pastor of Christ Presbyterian Church
and author of *Befriend* and *Irresistible Faith*

"Our church recently wrote a policy on sabbaticals, and I wish we had Rusty's book available to us then! Rusty has written a thoroughly compelling and theologically informed case for sabbaticals that is not only concise but comprehensive. Pastors and ministry leaders will benefit from the wealth of practical information he provides. I will not be surprised to find this book referenced more frequently as pastors seek to take time to break from the demands of ministry for renewal and refreshment."

Jonathan Holmes, Pastor of Counseling, Parkside
Church; Executive Director, Fieldstone Counseling

"While the world promotes, even rewards, a driven, multitasking, hurried, overworked lifestyle, Rusty McKie points church leaders to the grossly underestimated value of proactive rest. Rusty explains why a period of intentional rest, revitalization, and recalibration is anything but not productive downtime from work. Sabbatical rest is crucial for kingdom-minded, Spirit-led leadership. Don't miss taking advantage of this practical guide to enjoying the benefit of a meaningful sabbatical experience."

Bill Wellons, Co-founder of Fellowship Bible Church Little Rock, is the Executive Director of the Church Planting Leadership Residency at Fellowship Associates in Little Rock, Arkansas. He is the author of *Getting Away to Get It Together* and *What Matters Most!*

Praise for the "How-To" Series

"The Sojourn Network 'How-To' books are a great combination of biblical theology and practical advice, driven by a commitment to the gospel and the local congregation. Written by the local church for the local church — just the job!"

> **Tim Chester**, pastor of Grace Church Boroughbridge, faculty member of Crosslands Training, and author of over 40 books

"This series brings pastoral wisdom for everyday life in the church of Jesus Christ. Think of these short, practical books as the equivalent of a healthy breakfast, a sandwich and apple for lunch, and a family enjoying dinner together. The foundational theology is nutritious, and the practical applications will keep the body strong."

> **Dr. David Powlison**, Executive Director of CCEF; senior editor, Journal of Biblical Counseling; author of *Good and Angry: Redeeming Anger* and *Making All Things New: Restoring Joy to the Sexually Broken*

"Most leaders don't need another abstract book on leadership; we need help with the 'how-to's.' And my friends in the Sojourn Network excel in this area. I've been well served by their practical ministry wisdom, and I know you will be too."

> **Bob Thune**, Founding Pastor, Coram Deo Church, Omaha, NE, author of *Gospel Eldership* and co-author of *The Gospel-Centered Life*

"I cannot express strong enough what a valuable resource this is for church planters, church planting teams and young churches. The topics that are addressed in these books are so needed in young churches. I have been in ministry and missions for over 30 years and I learned a lot from reading. Very engaging and very practical!"

Larry McCrary, Co-Founder and Director of The Upstream Collective

"There are many aspects of pastoral ministry that aren't (and simply can't) be taught in seminary. Even further, many pastors simply don't have the benefit of a brotherhood of pastors that they can lean on to help them navigate topics such as building a healthy plurality of elders or working with artists in the church. I'm thankful for the men and women who labored to produce this series, which is both theologically-driven and practically-minded. The Sojourn Network "How-To" series is a great resource for pastors and church planters alike."

Jamaal Williams, Lead Pastor of Sojourn Midtown, Louisville, KY

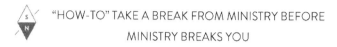 "HOW-TO" TAKE A BREAK FROM MINISTRY BEFORE
MINISTRY BREAKS YOU

Rusty S. McKie, Jr.

Series Editor: Dave Harvey

Sabbaticals
"How-To" Take a Break from Ministry before Ministry Breaks You

© 2018 Rusty S. McKie, Jr.
All rights reserved.

A publication of Sojourn Network Press in Louisville, KY. For more books by Sojourn Network, visit us at sojournnetwork.com/store.

Cover design: Josh Noom & Benjamin Vrbicek
Interior design: Benjamin Vrbicek

Trade paperback ISBN: 978-1732055261

Scripture quotations are from The ESV® Bible (The Holy Bible, English Standard Version®), copyright © 2001 by Crossway, a publishing ministry of Good News Publishers. 2016 Text Edition. Used by permission. All rights reserved.

All emphases in Scripture quotations have been added by the author.

The Sojourn Network book series is dedicated to the pastors, elders, and deacons of Sojourn Network churches. Because you are faithful, the church will be served and sent as we plant, grow, and multiply healthy churches that last.

CONTENTS

SERIES PREFACE

Why should the Sojourn Network publish a "How-To" series?

It's an excellent question, since it leads to a more personal and pertinent question for you: *Why should you bother to read any of these books?*

Sojourn Network, the ministry I am honored to lead, exists to plant, grow, and multiply healthy networks, churches, and pastors. Therefore, it seems only natural to convert some of our leader's best thinking and practices into written material focusing on the "How-To" aspects of local church ministry and multiplication.

We love church planters and church planting. But we've come to believe it's not enough to do assessments and fund church plants. We must also help, equip, and learn from one another in order to be good shepherds and leaders. We must stir up one another to the good work of leading churches towards their most fruitful future.

That's why some books will lend themselves to soul calibration for ministry longevity, while others will examine the riggings of specific ministries or specialized mission. This is essential work to building ministries *that last*. But God has also placed it on our hearts to share our mistakes and most fruitful practices so that others might improve upon what we have done. This way, everyone wins.

If our prayer is answered, this series will bring thoughtful, pastoral, charitable, gospel-saturated, church-grounded, renewal-based "practice" to the rhythms of local church life and network collaboration.

May these "How-To" guides truly serve you. May they arm you with new ideas for greater leadership effectiveness. Finally, may they inspire you to love Jesus more and serve his people with grace-inspired gladness, in a ministry that passes the test of time.

Dave Harvey
President, Sojourn Network

INTRODUCTORY LETTER

Dear Reader, you are not a machine.

When I was a teenager, I worked summers on my grandfather's farm in South Carolina. I know from experience that farming is grueling. I'm pretty sure that's why my Dad insisted I labor my summers away — to give me a holy motivation to do something other than farming.

Well done, Dad! Mission accomplished.

One particular job defined my temporary fling with farming: Clearing the fields for planting. Let me paint a picture for you. My cousin and I scoured open fields in 100-degree weather for ten hours a day digging up every rock and root. We did this monotonous labor until we cleared a field and then moved on to the next field. The most insulting part of the whole ordeal was what my uncle did next. He would till the soil of the cleared field to — you guessed it — unearth more rocks and roots. We would head back to the same field for another week or two. What's the definition of insanity again? Oh yeah, doing the same thing expecting different results.

I hated that job!

Now because my family members are a perceptive bunch and because they take delight in assigning nicknames that remind you of things you detest, I received my very own moniker that summer — "Root." To this day when my family sees me, their sun-worn faces crease from their big smiles as they say, "How's it going, Root?"

The first reason I share this story is to say that I come from a family of hard workers. Workaholism is not only something McKies do, it's in our blood. My journey toward embracing God's idea of rest has been a difficult one, and I felt like I was doing something wrong when I took my first sabbatical. Rest is difficult for me, and it's taken years to even know where to begin. Yet God has deconstructed assumptions and practices in my life because he loves me too much to allow me to kill myself from overworking. The process has been painful, and it's been good. I look forward to sharing more of my story with you.

The second reason I share my farming woes is to say that a life that honors Jesus requires cultivation. One of the temptations in ministry is to operate as if we're machines. We can think that faithful sacrifice to Jesus looks like saying yes to everything, pushing through and digging into more and more productivity. We get to work, and the expectations pile up (external and/or internal).

As a pastor, you are expected to work 114 hours a week,[1] produce a life-changing sermon every Sunday, grand slam

---

[1] Thom Rainer, "How many hours must a pastor work to satisfy the congregation?" https://thomrainer.com/2013/07/how-many-hours-must-a-pastor-work-to-satisfy-the-congregation.

leadership development, disciple twelve people just like Jesus, break down social and cultural barriers, network with other pastors in your city, build lasting friendships with non-Christians, take an annual international mission trip and all without neglecting your family or health. Then there are the rocks and roots of ministry. A church member lambasts you in an email. A friend disqualifies himself from ministry through moral failure. Your elder team is more dysfunctional than functional. Your marriage feels like a mess. Your parenting feels like a mess. You feel like a mess. You look at yourself in the mirror and don't recognize the person staring back at you.

When the serious stuff of life and ministry bangs us up, we are tempted to trudge on as if we're made of metal rather than flesh and bones. Our losses scream at us, yet we ignore them as we just keep working.

In the name of ministry, we can dehumanize ourselves. There are certain "rocks and roots" that need our attention and require us to slow down. We are reminded of our limits and must respect them. Our humanity is humbling, and humility demands we learn how to be still and let God be God (Psalm 46:10). What we are talking about here is longevity in ministry — cultivating a life that honors God in both our work and rest.

Enter sabbaticals — taking a break from ministry before ministry breaks you.

I want to introduce you to this friend of mine. My hope and prayer for you is that after reading this little book you'll have a better understanding of how to prepare for, take, and benefit from a sabbatical *so that* you might complete your ministry of testifying to the grace of King Jesus (Acts 20:23–24). But please do not think that a sabbatical is enough for you. Extended time away from ministry will not save or satisfy you. If you take a sabbatical without addressing the rocks and roots under the surface, then you'll burnout shortly after getting back to work. What we need in life are healthy rhythms. Because of this, we can't just talk about sabbaticals (macro-rest) but must also talk about sabbaths (micro-rest). More on this in the pages to come.

Speaking of what's to come, here is where we are headed:

Philosophy: A Theology of Work and Rest. What are sabbaticals? Are they biblical? Should pastors take sabbaticals when church members work just as hard? How should we think about them in relation to our work?

Principles: Preparing for a Sabbatical. What's the purpose? Who should take them? How do we pay for them? Who should be involved in the decision? How should it be communicated?

Process (Part 1): Taking a Sabbatical. What should you focus on during the sabbatical? What makes a sabbatical meaningful? What are the common challenges on a sabbatical? How do we navigate those challenges?

Process (Part 2): Returning from a Sabbatical. What should we expect? How do we get back into the swing of things? And most importantly, how do we integrate the principles of sabbaticals into our normal work rhythms?

If you are ready, let's get after it.

May you find true rest in Jesus,
Rusty S. McKie, Jr.
Lead Pastor of Sojourn Community Church in
Chattanooga, Tennessee

PHILOSOPHY

A THEOLOGY OF WORK AND REST

"School's out for summer
School's out forever"
— Alice Cooper

Do you remember that feeling as a child? Remember the anticipation of the last day of school, the build-up in the final hours and the explosion of joy as you ran out the school-doors into the wide-open possibilities of summer. Summer break meant adventure, sunshine, long days, and memorable nights. During the school year, we lived in black and white, but the summer was a technicolored dream.

Now do you remember the feeling as a newly-employed member of society? Remember the sinking realization and forceful imposition of reality that you would never get a summer break again. Recall the monochromatic lens inching down over your vision of life like a final curtain. But seriously, let's not become too melodramatic here. Our childhood summers were filled with just as much boredom as

excitement. Nostalgia takes the wheel and drives us down
memory lane, and we long for summer.

Now as adults, we work for the weekend,[1] labor for
Labor Day and tough it out to travel. We work toward breaks
in an effort to keep the nostalgia alive.

But why do we idealize rest?

The Principles beneath Sabbaticals

The idea for sabbaticals comes from passages in the Old
Testament about a seventh-year rest. On the seventh year,
farmers gave their land a break from producing (Exodus
23:10–11; Leviticus 25:1–7), slaves were redeemed from their
service (Exodus 21:2–6) and debts were canceled
(Deuteronomy 15:1–5). In order to obey this command, Israel
needed a big faith. For an agricultural society, giving the land
a sabbatical meant taking a sabbatical — not to mention
releasing your workers and canceling the income owed you.
The seventh-year meant trusting God to provide while not
taking care of business as usual. Many pastors have been
confronted with their need for such faith as they step away
for several months on a sabbatical. It's a humbling experience.

Yet can we in good conscience make a case for paid-
sabbaticals for pastors based off some random farming and
debt practices in ancient Israel?

We must keep digging beneath the surface. Our word
"sabbatical" is a transliteration from the Greek word
sabbatikos, which means "of the sabbath." We can't talk about

---

[1] The cultural anthropologists, Loverboy, have written with striking
clarity on this topic with their song *Everybody's Working for the Weekend*.

sabbaticals without talking about sabbaths because a sabbatical is an extended sabbath.

Leviticus 25:4 says, "in the seventh year there shall be a Sabbath of solemn rest for the land, a Sabbath to the LORD." In Leviticus 25:1–7, Moses calls the seventh year a "Sabbath" four times in seven verses. The repetition punctuated for Israel that this (a sabbatical year) is like that (a weekly sabbath). Moses applies the same verbiage and basic application of sabbath to a sabbatical year — interrupt your work with rest. Because of this, the biblical principles of rest found in passages about the sabbath can enlighten and inform other types of rest whether it be an hour, a day, a three-day retreat or a sabbatical.

What are these sabbath principles that inform other types of rest?

Rest is Grounded in Creation

> Remember the Sabbath day, to keep it holy. Six days you shall labor, and do all your work, but the seventh day is a Sabbath to the LORD your God . . . For in six days the LORD made heaven and earth, the sea, and all that is in them, and rested on the seventh day. Therefore the LORD blessed the Sabbath day and made it holy. (Exodus 20:8–11)

Principle 1 — We rest because we are human and not God.

Much of our exhaustion and stress in the work of pastoral ministry can be traced back to our tendency to forget our humanity. The weight of the world produces ulcers in our stomachs because we subconsciously attempt to play God.[2] In God's long-suffering love toward us, he commands us to

Workaholism is ultimately a worship problem. rest because he knows the gravitational pull inside us to try to "be like God" (Genesis 3:4). Workaholism is ultimately a worship problem.[3] Rather than imaging God — who worked six days and rested on the seventh — we kill ourselves with illusions of omni-competence. However, God who did not need rest took a break to enjoy the goodness of his work.

What a wise Maker we follow!

Pastors and church planters, hear me: You are not God, and Jesus doesn't expect you to be. God models stepping back and enjoying the goodness of the work you've done. God's work and rest rhythm in Genesis 2:1–3 is like a plumb line for our lives. As humans created in God's image and as Christians recreated in Jesus' image, we are made to work hard for Jesus and rest well in Jesus. If we do not submit ourselves to this creation principle, then we will deny our humanity on either point of working without rest or resting without work.

---

[2] For more on this idea of attempting to play God through ministry and suffering the consequences of stress, see Zack Eswine's *The Imperfect Pastor* as well as Hannah Anderson's *Humble Roots*.

[3] Eric Geiger, "4 Ways to Fight Being a Ministry Workaholic," https://ericgeiger.com/2016/11/4-ways-to-fight-being-a-ministry-workaholic. "Work is a gift, and work ethic resides in men and women of character, but in our idolatry, we can easily make work our god. Pastors have warned me, 'Ministry can be a great place to hide out and a great place to burn out.' Ministry can be a haven for the workaholic. In most jobs overwork feels sinful and neglectful, but when serving in ministry, overwork can wrongly feel holy."

Ultimately, this principle demands *humility* to embrace our limits and losses. In a culture that capitalizes on strength, this rhythm is hard to develop. Pastors and church planters, Jesus is not embarrassed by your limitations, you shouldn't be either.

Rest is Grounded in Redemption

> Observe the Sabbath day, to keep it holy, as the LORD your God commanded you. Six days you shall labor and do all your work, but the seventh day is a Sabbath to the LORD your God . . . You shall remember that you were a slave in the land of Egypt, and the LORD your God brought you out from there with a mighty hand and an outstretched arm. Therefore the LORD your God commanded you to keep the Sabbath day. (Deuteronomy 5:12–15)

Principle 2 — We rest because we are free and no longer slaves.

For years, my day off was the most miserable day of my week. I loved being with my family, but I struggled mentally to be with my family.

During work, I rode the dragon of the week doing my best to tame that mythical beast. I ran (sometimes literally) from meeting to meeting — rejoicing with those who rejoiced, mourning with those who mourn, playing my role as a mediator to conflicts, pouring into potential leaders, speaking encouraging truths and, when necessary, hard ones too. During my early years of planting our church, I burned the proverbial candle at both ends. I met people for breakfast, lunch, dinner, and hung out until the wee hours of early morning. Slept a couple hours. Dragged my carcass out of bed. Raised the dead with a cup of coffee. And did it all again. Oh yeah, I also had to write sermons, create systems, plan for the future, and do administrative work.

Let me be clear: This is not a humble brag or a busyness badge of faithfulness. I share a snapshot of my pace in those early years with some shame. I was not running in such a way to win the prize (1 Corinthians 9:24); I was running scared.[4] I was working beyond my limits, and I was enslaved. I had a pharaoh inside me cracking a whip and screaming, "Make more bricks, slave!" Work was my master, but it was also my drug of choice. I was addicted to the adrenaline rush, and my day off was empirical evidence that I was a junkie.

When I stopped working, my mind continued to labor.

Ever been there?

I was like a jar of river water.[5] As long as I kept active, the murky water hid what was inside. Once I stopped, the sediment settled, and a deep sadness came into focus. Then I felt bad about feeling bad. This was my family day when my wife and kids were supposed to have my undivided attention. This, my friends, is what we call slavery.

In Deuteronomy, Moses gives God's rest command for the second time. However, this time, he does not ground the command in creation but in redemption. Rest because you are no longer slaves! Pete Scazzero puts it so well when he says,

---

[4] Are you running scared? There's a book for that by Ed Welch called *Running Scared: Fear, Worry and the God of Rest.*

[5] Illustration taken from Ruth Haley Barton, *Invitation to Solitude and Silence: Experiencing God's Transformative Presence* (Downers Grove: IVP Books, 2010), 29–30.

"Work requires something of us; it depletes our energies, our wisdom, our reserves. If we don't allow the soil of our souls to rest, we do violence to ourselves."[6]

Pastor, Jesus broke the chains of your slavery. Your identity is not found in your work but in the work of Christ. You can clock out as you collapse on the floor with your small kids because Jesus sustains you and your church. Because of Jesus, you can listen and fully engage your wife as she recounts her day. You can stop thinking about the crisis at church and enjoy your time off because Jesus is the Redeemer! He redeems your rest, and through rest, he redeems you.

Rest is Grounded in New Creation

> For if Joshua had given them rest, God would not have spoken of another day later on. So then, there remains a Sabbath rest for the people of God, for whoever has entered God's rest has also rested from his works as God did from his. Let us therefore strive to enter that rest, so that no one may fall by the same sort of disobedience. (Hebrews 4:8–11)

Principle 3 — We rest because we are sojourners and have not arrived.

God's invitation to work and rest is an open door to reclaim our humanity. We are prone to return to slavery and

---

[6] Pete Scazzero, *The Emotionally Healthy Leader: How Transforming Your Inner Life Will Deeply Transform Your Church, Team, and the World* (Grand Rapids: Zondervan, 2015), 164.

imbalance — to convince ourselves that our previous bondage was good (Exodus 16:3). And so, the author of Hebrews tells us we must work to enter God's rest. Put in practical terms, we will never arrive this side of heaven in terms of experiencing a perfect work-life balance. In fact, the idea of a *work-life balance* has confiscated much ink as of late. Everyone, from Christian to non-Christian, is trying to figure out the mysterious formula. Some have even rejected the idea all-together saying it's impossible because it's an illusion.[7]

I get it. We get away to rest and can't stop thinking about work. We get into the office only to daydream about the weekend. We will strike a work-life balance, but that life will be found wrapped up in Christ in the Resurrected life to come. Friends, there is a future Sabbath rest coming, but we're not home yet. We are on this journey toward a new creation where all our work and all our rest will be a perfect expression of praise and worship to King Jesus as we reign with him (Romans 8:16–17; Galatians 4:6–7).

Until then, we work for Jesus, and we work to rest in him. This reorients our understanding of a work-life balance. It's not as if work is what we do in order to live our life. The loving gift that God gives is fullness of life in both our work and our rest (John 10:10). The author of Hebrews reminds us that we are sojourners in process of figuring all this out, but he also reminds us that Joshua could not give rest. Only the better Joshua can — his name is Jesus. Jesus our true Sabbath Rest.

---

[7] Jessica Lutz, "It's Time to Kill the Fantasy That Is Work-Life Balance," https://www.forbes.com/sites/jessicalutz/2018/01/11/its-time-to-kill-the-fantasy-that-is-work-life-balance/#1f2b71d670a1.

Jesus, our Sabbath Rest

> And he said to them, "The Sabbath was made for man,
> not man for the Sabbath. So the Son of Man is lord even
> of the Sabbath." (Mark 2:27–28)

Principle 4 — We rest in Jesus because he is our life.

Jesus' practice of healing on the sabbath is one of the details that got him killed (Mark 3:16; John 5:1–16; Luke 13:10–17; John 9:1–7, 17). However, I think there's more going on here than Jesus trying to pick a fight with the Pharisees.

> **Jesus healed so often on the sabbath to show us that some healing only comes through rest.**

Could it be that Jesus healed so often on the sabbath *in order to* show us that some healing only comes through rest?[8]

Jesus is Lord of the sabbath, and sabbath was made for man. The work of making disciples with Jesus is exhilarating (Matthew 28:18–20). But remember, we have limits. Jesus modeled how to navigate limits by getting away from his own work in ministry (Mark 1:35–36; 6:46; Luke 5:16; 6:12; John

---

[8] This insight was taken from John Mark Comer's *Garden City: Work, Rest, and the Art of Being Human* (Grand Rapids: Zondervan, 2015), 227–229. "Now, as I said earlier, it's easy to misread stories like this, as if the main point is the Sabbath is a bad, legalistic rule that we have to abandon. That's missing the heart of the story. Jesus was known far and wide as a healer. Healing is a tangible expression of the inbreaking kingdom of God. But did you know that almost all of Jesus' healings take place on the Sabbath? I don't think that's a coincidence. Why? Because the Sabbath is a day for healing. That was true in the first century, and I would argue it's true today. Jesus does some of his best work on the Sabbath."

6:15). Pastor, Jesus loves you enough to promote and promise rest (Matthew 11:28). He wants to meet you in that rest and heal your weariness. He wants to remind you that he builds his church when you're working and when you're resting. He wants you to be confident that even the powers of hell can't stop him (Matthew 16:18–19). He wants your work and rest to be so dependent on him that you conclude, *I am hidden in Christ, and he is my life* (Colossians 3:3–4).

Honoring Jesus by depending on him with your work and rest is good for you. It's also good for your church. They need to see you working hard and resting well to the glory of God. And if you are able, they need to see you take a sabbatical as a declaration that you are not God, you are not a slave, you have not arrived, and Jesus is your life.

Perceptions of Sabbaticals

A Congregation's Unbiblical Perception of Sabbaticals

"Why should my pastor get a paid-sabbatical? I work hard too but don't get a sabbatical." Some church members don't understand sabbaticals. This can especially be true for businessmen and women as well as older congregants. If you're reading this as a church member or lay leader, let me speak to you for a moment. There are at least two reasons why sabbaticals are an appropriate gift to offer your pastor.

First, sabbaticals are appropriate because pastoral ministry is unlike other jobs. If you are not a paid-pastor at your church, I pray you become more aware of the challenges your pastor faces so that you can pray for him and champion sabbaticals for him. Most pastors will not tell you the difficulties he and his family face; so let me share for him. For starters, consider Thom Rainer's five reasons why pastors should take sabbaticals:[9]

1. A pastor has emotional highs and lows unlike most other vocations.
2. A pastor is on 24-hour call.
3. Pastors need time of uninterrupted study.
4. Pastors who have sabbaticals have longer tenure at churches.
5. Pastors who have sabbaticals view the time off as an affirmation from their churches.

I am not saying that church members don't have stressful jobs, but I am saying pastoring is particularly stressful. Those who choose to answer the call to ministry have a common bond. Most folks in our churches live on a three-legged stool composed of their spiritual, professional, and family life. If one of those legs wobbles, they have two others they can lean on. For pastors, however, those three things tend to merge into a single leg. When you sit on a one-legged stool, it takes more concentration and energy. Those in ministry can teeter on the edge of balance exhausted by the experience. Sadly, many fall, which in turn has a crippling effect on our faith, our family, and our ministries. What I'm saying is this, the physical, emotional, and spiritual endurance needed for

---

[9] Thom Rainer, "Five Reasons Your Pastor Should Take A Sabbatical," https://thomrainer.com/2014/02/five-reasons-your-pastor-should-take-a-sabbatical/.

pastoral ministry is unique — especially when considering they will stand before God and give an account for how they led (Hebrews 13:7). Talk about a dreaded performance review!

To illustrate the uniqueness of pastoring, pastors are like the Special Ops of the Kingdom. Please hear me: I'm not trying to reinforce an unhealthy divide between the sacred and secular. If you nanny, run a fortune five-hundred company, craft lattes, or cultivate souls as a stay-at-home parent, then you are a Kingdom Ambassador on mission for the King (2 Corinthians 5:16–20). Your work matters. Keep up the good work for Jesus (Colossians 3:17)!

But do understand that pastors are like Navy Seals on the front lines of the battle. They do hard work and bear psychological burdens for the sake of the church that the church does not even see. There's the stress of navigating actual danger, but there's also the anxiety of potential danger. There are disasters your church has avoided that you'll never know about because your pastors did their job. On top of this, there's the emotional roller coaster of rejoicing with those who rejoice, weeping with those who weep, receiving positive feedback for a job well done and collecting attacks for mistakes or failures. And some days, all this happens before lunch. Finally, if a congregant has a moral failure, they most likely will keep their job. For pastors, disqualification means a lost job.

The weightiness of that last sentence is important to feel. If Satan can take out an under-shepherd (1 Peter 5:1–4), then the flock of God suffers. This means pastors have a unique target on their back. The spiritual warfare and demonic attack on a pastor and his family can be overwhelming.

Pastoring is a calling, and called men rejoice in both the joys and difficulties of it. The job is brutal and beautiful, and it's unlike anything else. In light of this, sabbaticals are a welcome gift that would benefit many tired pastors.

Second, sabbaticals are appropriate because of the benefits they offer everyone. Sabbaticals are on the rise in the business world. *The Harvard Business Review* points out the rising trend in that 17% of companies in 2017 offered sabbaticals to their employees. *HBR* not only acknowledges but endorses the trend because of the benefits to the employee and organization as a whole.[10] *Forbes* also praises the benefits of sabbaticals for employees whether the sabbatical focuses primarily on personal rest, further study for the

> **God is honored when a pastor loves to pour out his life for the church and when the church loves to honor their pastor.**

organization or even humanitarian work. Their conclusion: the employee taking a sabbatical is refreshed, and subordinates grow while covering new responsibilities for their direct report. The final result is more collaboration and shared leadership once the employee returns from a sabbatical.[11] If REI, Zillow, and Intel see the wisdom in

---

[10] David Burkus, "Research Shows That Organizations Benefit When Employees Take Sabbaticals," https://hbr.org/2017/08/research-shows-that-organizations-benefit-when-employees-take-sabbaticals.

[11] Judy Nelson, "Do You Need A Sabbatical?" https://www.forbes.com/sites/forbescoachescouncil/2017/10/16/do-you-need-a-sabbatical/#291009d22f14.

offering employees paid sabbaticals,[12] then shouldn't the church? Heck, the wisdom came out of our Bible!

There is a sacred dance between a pastor and his church here. God is honored when a pastor loves to pour out his life for the church and when the church loves to honor their pastor. God loves this other-centered giving and receiving displayed in sabbaticals as a congregation, like Jesus, "in humility counts others more significant than yourselves" (Philippians 2:3).[13]

A Pastor's Unbiblical Perception of Sabbaticals

I've noticed in general that older pastors are less likely to even think about taking a sabbatical while younger pastors act as if sabbaticals are their God-given right. While I'm making gross stereotypes, let me make one more: the older generation of pastors have been characterized by sacrificing their family at the altar of ministry, while the younger has sacrificed ministry at the altar of their family. Now, I am not concerned as much with the validity of the stereotype as I am with what the stereotype tells us. My point is that we stereotype pastors because they model two real extremes in pastoral life — workaholism and laziness. In order to understand pastoral perceptions on sabbaticals, we need to comprehend what's under the hood of these extremes.

---

[12] Amanda Kreuser, "One Underused Perk That Keeps Top Talent Happy and Productive at Work," https://www.inc.com/amanda-pressner-kreuser/9-companies-with-incredible-sabbatical-policies.html.

[13] In fact, considering others more significant than yourself is a rhythm as old as eternity since God the Father, Son and Holy Spirit live in this sacred dance.

First, workaholism and laziness are built on a lie. Workaholism is built on the lie that our identity, worth, and a fulfilling life is found in work. Everything that gets in the way of productivity and career is therefore a curse. Similarly, pastoral laziness is built on the lie that our identity, worth, and a fulfilling life is found outside work. Work is seen as a curse keeping us from real life. The Creation story teaches us the truth that while work includes a curse, work is not cursed (Genesis 3:17–19). We are workers created in the image of a working God (Genesis 1:26–28). Workaholic and lazy pastors deny their image-bearing role by either ignoring God-honoring work or rest.

Second, workaholism and laziness drift into pride. Both of these struggles drift into the pride of performance or entitlement, and both are enemies of grace.[14] Workaholics work as if they don't need the rest that a sabbatical provides. Companies in the business world call sabbaticals a benefit. In the church, we should call them what they are — a gift of grace from God. You can't earn grace, you simply receive the gift. A performance-driven mentality is prideful because there's no way we could earn the gift God gives for free.

On the other hand, the lazy pastor feels entitled to a sabbatical because he thinks he deserves it. But there is nothing worthy in us or in our work that necessitates we get a sabbatical. In fact, the privilege of leading in Jesus' church is far more than we deserve. Our calling is a gift. Our pastoral abilities and competencies are a gift. Our jobs are a gift. And a sabbatical is an undeserved gift (1 Corinthians 4:7). Many

---

[14] Daniel Montgomery and Mike Cosper, *Faithmapping: A Gospel Atlas for Your Spiritual Journey* (Wheaton: Crossway, 2013), 74–76.

churches have failed to even think through sabbatical policies, and their pastors must press on. Some churches wish they could fully fund their pastor's sabbatical, yet their resources don't match their desire. If you're able to take a sabbatical, make sure your attitude is fueled by gratitude to God and your church rather than entitlement.

A Biblical Perception of Sabbaticals

If we're honest, both of these extremes live in us. In the span of an hour, we can work like we have no limits and then rest like the world owes us. Which is why, the answer to our sickness is not working less or working more. Grace is the only medicine that can cure a sin-sick soul. When our identity, worth, and life is found in Jesus, then we can work and rest as God intended (1 Corinthians 15:10; Philippians 3:7–8). Keeping Jesus in his appropriate place puts our perceptions of sabbaticals in their appropriate place.

> We cannot earn nor do we deserve sabbaticals, but they are a gift of grace.

We cannot earn nor do we deserve sabbaticals, but they are a gift of grace. And grace is a Person. Grace is the generosity of Jesus experienced. Through sabbaticals, Jesus offers us an extended stay in his weariness-healing presence. Through deliberate time away from ministry, Jesus ministers to us. We were not created *for* work-alone (workaholism) or *for* rest-alone (laziness), but we were created *for* Christ-alone. In him, our work and rest are held together (Colossians 1:16–17). In him, we find our life.

If you are eager to learn more about how to enter into this season of rest, then let's keep trucking as we turn our attention to preparing for a sabbatical.

PRINCIPLES

PREPARING FOR A SABBATICAL

"I can show you the world
Shining, shimmering splendid"
– Aladdin

Before Aladdin and Jasmine jumped on a magic carpet to sing *A Whole New World* (and thereafter burn that song into our cerebral cortex), the prince had to convince the princess. Aladdin promised to rescue Jasmine from her unsatisfactory life and to show her a new, shining and shimmering world of refreshment. He held out his hand and said, "Do you trust me?" She did. They soared. They saw. They sang.

But here's the problem.

He was not a prince.

Even with the life-coaching of Genie to "be yourself," Aladdin lied about who he was *in order to* show Jasmine a whole new world. Pastor, there are countless pseudo-princes out there promising you a whole new world. They hold out a hand offering rest, taking you on a ride and when life gets rough, they chastise, *Don't you dare close your eyes!*

Jesus is the true King, and he means it when he promises, "Come to me, all who labor and are heavy laden, and I will give you rest" (Matthew 11:28). He holds out a hand for us to find our rest in him. To enter this rest, we must trust him. Instead of "Don't you dare close your eyes!" Jesus' word to us is, "Hold your breath, it gets better!" The decision to go on a sabbatical and the preparation process takes steps of faith. Those steps result in a policy, a proposal, and a church-wide sending.

A Sabbatical Policy

You need a policy before you need a sabbatical. As you write a policy, consider the following questions and observations to help your leadership create a policy that best fits your context:

Who should get sabbaticals? Some churches only give their lead pastor sabbaticals. Others give all paid-pastors sabbaticals. Others even provide sabbaticals for key paid staff members.

How often should a sabbatical be? Churches tend to offer sabbaticals every five or seven years, with the trend moving toward every five years.

How long should the sabbatical be? Time allotments are between one to six months with three months being the most common. Three months tends to fit nicely into a church's summer calendar which is typically a less demanding period of the year. Those taking sabbaticals should expect it will take around a month to detox from work. The second and third month is where meaningful insights begin to occur. Some churches offer sabbaticals with a stipulation that part of the time is spent on a project that directly or indirectly benefits the church (more on this under types of sabbaticals).

Before I go any further, I want to state that it's not my goal to give you a cookie-cutter policy here. My desire is to get your team talking — about how loving generosity toward your pastor, stewardship of resources, and practical creativity come together to create a culture in your church that displays the gospel to the world.

Should the church help fund sabbaticals? While some churches may provide grant options for sabbaticals, some may find financial contribution difficult depending on the size of the church (more to come on how to fund your sabbatical in the next section).

When should the proposal be submitted? Setting a date ensures good stewardship that will help prepare the church and staff for an upcoming sabbatical. Many churches require proposals to be submitted anywhere from six months to a year with the option for postponement given the needs of the church.

Who should approve your proposal? If your church has a plurality of pastors, they would approve your proposal. However if your church does not, then you will want to specify a group in your policy. This group should love you and the church enough to make decisions that benefit everyone. The point of this group is to set you up for success on your sabbatical as well as for the longevity of your ministry. They are not angling to get away with giving you the least amount of rest you need but instead providing outside counsel to help you get the maximum benefit out of your sabbatical.

When will you give a post-sabbatical report? It is wise to let your leaders and the church hear how the sabbatical benefited you so that they see a return on their investment. This can be as simple as sharing in a staff meeting or a member meeting. In the policy, focus more on *who* you are sharing with than *when* you will share. No one knows the future. The best time to share will be clear to you and your leaders once you are back.

These are the types of questions you want to answer in creating a policy. Check out Appendix 1 for example policies.

A Sabbatical Proposal

A sabbatical proposal should include the type of sabbatical, the general purpose of your sabbatical, the specific goals, and the plan for your sabbatical.

Types of Sabbaticals

There are four types of sabbaticals.[1] *First, there is a working sabbatical.* This is similar to what a professor in higher education would take. The church grants an extended period

---

[1] I would argue the first two are not technically sabbaticals since they are a reallocation of work. However, they are worth including here because people often mislabel them.

of time to work on a larger project (examples: a writing project, research for a building campaign, finalizing a doctoral thesis, etc.). Your plan will reflect how your hours will be spent as well as include goals you hope to hit along the way. This is a reallocation of work hours rather than a sabbatical.

Second, there is a serving sabbatical. This is an extended period to grow in an area of ministry, not by leading but through serving. The church grants you time to go overseas or across the street with a local non-profit. The purpose can range from personal development to participating in a non-profit with the goal of future partnership. Similar to a working sabbatical, your plan will include how your hours will be spent but will also include a plan for funding. Since the time away does not include rest, labeling this as a sabbatical would be a misrepresentation of a sabbatical.

Third, there is a refreshment sabbatical. Now we are in the territory of a true sabbatical. The church grants time away from the pressures of ministry for their pastor to recalibrate with God, family, and friends. The plan for this type of sabbatical is as varied as the individuals taking them. The next section will be dedicated to crafting your plan for a refreshment sabbatical. The benefits to the church are more intangible but nonetheless real and lasting, because health tends to slide downhill. A healthy, refreshed pastor with a renewed hunger for ministry airs out the stagnate rooms of a church upon his return.

Fourth, there is a refreshment sabbatical with a work/educational component. As mentioned above, some churches want a professional component included. In this case, you are combining a working and a refreshment sabbatical. In reality, this means you need to create a personal and professional plan to reflect both. When it comes to your actual time away, separate your time between these as much as possible by fronting your personal refreshment and completing it with your professional development (or vice versa). Rest when you rest; work when you work.

In *Leading on Empty*, Wayne Cordeiro argues a "good sabbatical plan includes opportunities for learning."[2] But he warns:

> The educational component, however, should only compromise one-third of the sabbatical. Two-thirds of the time should be cordoned off for a true sabbatical rest — where your vitality is restored with plenty of R&R as well as doing the things that fill your tank.[3]

The General Purpose of Your Refreshment Sabbatical

The general purpose of every sabbatical is refreshment *in order to* return to your church with a renewed vision for life and ministry. We shouldn't breeze past this point.

The general purpose of every sabbatical is refreshment to return to your church with renewed vision for life and ministry.

We live in a pragmatic culture, and it's seeped into our churches. This shapes our work and rest. We debate questions like: Is gospel-centered ministry marked by faithfulness or fruitfulness?

---

[2] Wayne Cordeiro, *Leading on Empty: Refilling Your Tank and Renewing Your Passion* (Minneapolis: Bethany House, 2009), 130.

[3] Ibid.

Think about that — we conclude healthy ministry is either determined by my faithfulness (which boils down to what I do) or by my fruitfulness (which is displayed in what I produce). While both our faithfulness and fruitfulness are a result of healthy ministry, they are not the final judge. This is why we mislabel working sabbaticals *because* we think a sabbatical (like our work) is only valuable if they *produce* a tangible profit for our church. This is a very Western way of thinking. If we're not careful, we can downplay the benefits God values. The confusion of health as productivity misses the central foundation of healthy work and rest — communion with Christ.

Listen, I love it when I am living up to my full potential and bringing others along. I desire our church to thrive with efficient productivity for the expansion of the Kingdom of God. But Jesus told us we can accomplish a lot of things apart from him, and yet apart from him "you can do nothing" (John 15:5). Healthy work and rest begin *not* with our productivity but with the productivity of Jesus upholding, sustaining, and bearing fruit through us as we abide in him (John 15:1–5). If we miss this point, then fruitless seasons in ministry or faithless seasons of personal failure or weakness will crush us. If communion with Jesus is not central to our sabbatical, then a sabbatical will induce a massive identity crisis (which is why refreshment-driven sabbaticals are so good for us; they force us to face our idols of work, ministry, and accomplishment). Communion with Jesus leads us to a place where we believe as singer-songwriter Ryan O'Neal sings, "Gold, silver or bronze hold no value here, where work and rest are equally revered."[4]

How to Decide the Specific Goals of Your Refreshment Sabbatical

In some seasons of life your sabbatical goals will slap you in the face. This was my experience. By the time our policy said I could have a sabbatical, my wife and I were overwhelmed with grief and ministry. We moved to plant our church pregnant with our first child, only to miscarry in the midst of unpacked boxes. A year later, we welcomed our firstborn son into the family and launched services on Easter. The following Thursday, I got a call from my mother-in-law that my wife's younger brother unexpectedly passed away. The three years that followed were filled with a growing church with normal growing pains and a personal heartache over unexplained infertility.

To be clear, Jesus did amazing work in our church — non-Christians came to know Jesus, the broken found healing, and those who had sworn off church became vital family members. But that was part of our problem. The whiplash from new life to sudden death and back again disoriented us. We kept pressing in and kept showing up. We put smiles on our faces when we wanted to cry and celebrated with others when we wanted to mourn for ourselves. We weren't being disingenuous; we just did what we signed up for — planting and pastoring a church. Choosing to consider

---

[4] Sleeping at Last, Lyrics to "Three." *Atlas: Year Two,* 2018, http://www.sleepingatlast.com/blog/2017/11/17/three.

others rather than ourselves was a saving grace in that difficult season of our life (Philippians 2:3). But as time went on, grief compounded and depression took form.

My goals became clear: 1) I was growing bitter in my grief and needed to do business with Jesus. 2) I also lacked a sense of connection with my family and wanted to be present with them. 3) Finally, we just wanted joy — we wanted the heaviness of life and ministry to be replaced with a sense of the heaviness of God's glory and grandeur. My plan then flooded out of these goals.

You still may be wondering though — *How do I decide my specific sabbatical goals?*

Three questions can help:

1. What do I need?
2. What do I want?
3. What do others say?

These questions help you discern from different angles what refreshment will look like for you. However, we all need help with these questions, and that's okay. Invite your leadership team, close friends and/or family members to offer honest input on your ideas, as well as their own suggestions. Be humble, and listen. Listen for themes. Discuss potential goals. Receive and pray through their feedback. Then start planning.

How to Create the Plan for Your Refreshment Sabbatical

Now that you have some goals in mind, it's time to start your plan. A well-rounded proposal will include refreshment in the following seven areas of life.

1. Reorder — How will your schedule promote refreshment?

You are about to embark in a new way of living for a couple months, and that's the point. This sabbatical is an intense fast from certain work and an intense feast on rest *in order to* bring about refreshment. Outline what your new rhythms will be during your sabbatical:

What will your daily, weekly and monthly rhythms be?

What will you fast? Obviously work. But what are the things that drag you back into work? Do you need to take a break from social media? Entertainment? Food/drink? Should you attend another church during your sabbatical? Bottom line: Put off as many energy depleting tasks as possible.

What will you feast on? Obviously rest. But what does rest look like for you? I hate mowing grass — so much so that I take every opportunity to tell people. But you may love cultivating your yard. Rest is subjective. What activities are life-giving? Increase those as much as possible *in order to* experience refreshment. But also recognize that all rest is not created equal. Watching a TV show might be restful but binging *The West Wing* for a week straight without spending any time with Jesus will not refresh your soul.

2. Revive — How will your soul care promote refreshment?

Paul warned Timothy, "Keep a close watch on yourself and on the teaching. Persist in this, for by so doing you will save both yourself and your hearers" (1 Timothy 4:16). Personal soul care is essential to pastoral ministry, and only Jesus can revive your soul. No true refreshment comes apart from drawing deep from the fountain of living water (Jeremiah 2:13; John 4:13–14). This "drinking" needs to be a daily practice. Plan this time wisely.

> **Personal soul care is essential to pastoral ministry, and only Jesus can revive your soul.**

- How much time will you spend with Jesus each day in Word and in prayer?
- What book/books of the Bible will you read, meditate on, and study?
- Are there any books beyond the Bible that will help you achieve your specific sabbatical goals? (Make sure books you choose help you focus on refreshment and soul care; this is not the time to read those new leadership books you've had on the back burner. See Appendix 2 for recommendations.)
- Will you journal and how often (see Appendix 3 on journaling)?
- Will you get professional counseling or set up times during your sabbatical to talk with a friend/mentor? If so, how often?

- Are there any other spiritual disciplines you will practice?

To give an example of what this could look like, here's what I did during my sabbatical. I committed to at least an hour a day in Word and prayer. I studied the book of Job in depth to help me process my bitterness and grief. I read *The Emotionally Healthy Leader* by Pete Scazzero and journaled every day (which was a new practice for me). My wife was my conversation partner for what I was processing during our sabbatical.

3. Rejuvenate — How will your health promote refreshment?

A lack of exercise combined with staring at a computer screen, never-ending sitting, deficient vitamin D, constant meal meetings, pastoral stress and spiritual warfare all add to — how should I say this — a physical and psychological beat down. Studies are crystal clear that we need exercise to feel physically and emotionally stable.[5] Yet pastors fall prey to self-destructive rhythms.

Your sabbatical is a chance to realign your physical health. There should be times during your sabbatical, when — as Mike Cosper says — we "do not plan on counting calories, carbs, sugars, or any other nonsense."[6] However, a sabbatical is not an exercise in excess. Consider if you need to change

---

[5] David Murray, *Reset: Living a Grace-Paced Life in a Burnout Culture* (Wheaton: Crossway, 2017), 78–83.

[6] Mike Cosper, *Recapturing the Wonder: Transcendent Faith in a Disenchanted World* (Downers Grove: IVP Books, 2017), 133.

your diet during your sabbatical.[7] Reclaim healthy sleeping patterns.[8] Decide what types of exercise you will incorporate into your sabbatical. For me, the stress of processing grief during my sabbatical meant I needed a physical outlet. I did some physical activity for an hour every day, and it was a lifesaving gift from God.

4. Recreate — How will fun promote refreshment?

First, consider hobbies. Is there a hobby you've always wanted to try? Now is the time. Take a photography class. Learn Jiu-Jitsu. Listen to records from start to finish. Try your hand at woodworking or learning an instrument. Is there a current hobby you wish you could spend more time on? Then get after it!

Second, consider vacations/family outings. This raises a really important question for you as an individual: Do you need to get out of your normal spaces to truly rest and achieve your sabbatical goals? When a soldier is on the front lines for too long, they receive a leave to get away. They retreat to another space to allow the fog of war to settle, gain some perspective and reenter the battle afresh. I needed this. We couldn't afford to get away the entire time. However, right out of the gate, we took a road trip to camp out West. Then we stayed home for a while, took a second trip to the beach and then wrapped up our sabbatical at home. Those trips helped me be present to my family and Jesus. (I'll talk more in a moment about how to fund your trips.)

---

[7] David Murray's chapter "Refuel" is a great guide for processing diet. Murray, *Reset,* 141–156.

[8] See also chapter on "Rest." Murray, *Reset,* 53–70.

Third, consider reading for fun. What types of books are an escape for you? If you can, connect your reading to one of your specific sabbatical goals. I'm about to reveal something about myself that is pretty geeky. I love reading about theoretical physics — specifically the field of study known as quantum gravity. To help move toward my third goal of gaining a sense of the heaviness of God's glory and grandeur, I picked up Carlo Rovelli's *Seven Brief Lessons on Physics.* I will never forget the awe I felt under the Colorado stars while reading, "In the 1930s, however, precise measurements by astronomers of the nebulae — small whitish clouds between the stars — showed that the Galaxy itself is a speck of dust in a huge cloud of galaxies, which extends as far as the eye can see using even our most powerful telescopes. The world has now become a uniform and boundless expanse."[9] I felt so small in the grandness of the cosmos, and yet so loved by my Father who sent his Son to die for me. My point is let your reading contribute to your overall refreshment (and it wouldn't hurt to read some physics *because physics is fascinating.*)

5. Reconnect — How will your relationships promote refreshment?

We have already thought through how we will connect with Jesus, but what about friends and family? If you are married and have children, then think through ways to create meaningful time and memories with them. Beyond your immediate family, will you spend time with your extended

---

[9] Carlo Rovelli, *Seven Brief Lessons on Physics* (New York: Riverhead Books, 2014), 27–28.

family? If so how much time? When and where? How does that support your sabbatical goals?

Are there any friends you want to reconnect with now that you have some more time on your hands? If so, put it in your plan, and communicate your expectations to them as clearly as possible before your sabbatical. However, let me give you two warnings regarding relationships and your sabbatical.

First, don't connect with extended family or friends because you feel obligated to do so. Your profession is people. That doesn't mean that people are projects; it means you live with people day in and out. It's okay if you and your immediate family want or need to step back from relationships during your sabbatical. Spend time with friends and extended family who refresh you.

Second, communicate conversation boundaries before spending time together. You need the ability in your relationships to pause a conversation and say, "You know this is making me think about ministry, and I'm starting to work in my head. Could we talk about something else?" With a clear and preparatory conversation before your sabbatical, you can speak like this without sounding like a jerk.

6. Refinance — How will your money promote refreshment?

How do we pay for sabbaticals? I hope this isn't disappointing, but you must get creative and industrious. Crafting a sabbatical proposal beforehand helps because you start pricing out how much it will cost you. From there consider the following options:

First, apply for grants and other opportunities. Head onto your favorite online search engine and type in "Free sabbatical grants for pastors" to see what's available to you. You can also search "Free places for pastors to stay" for nonprofits that provide free or affordable retreats for pastors and their families.[10] In addition, many denominations and monasteries provide free or affordable retreat lodging. You will do well to request grants and places to stay at least a year in advance since many of these programs fill up.

Second, ask your church for financial aid. If your church's policy allows, request funds for your sabbatical. Every pastor wants the church they serve to flourish with generosity, and a culture of generosity should never exclude their pastor and his family. Every five to seven years, the church gets to show their pastor in a big way how much they love and support him, not only by granting a sabbatical but also through alleviating financial stress during the sabbatical.

> **Every pastor wants the church they serve to flourish with generosity, and a culture of generosity should never exclude their pastor and his family.**

Third, save and be frugal. Knowing a sabbatical is coming five to seven years down the road means you can start saving for it. Setting up a separate sabbatical account at your bank is a good investment in the longevity of ministry. However, you also can get creative in making trips cheaper. We camped on our road trip out West in order to save money. In the moment, it wasn't the most comfortable, but the memories we have from that trip were worth it.

---

[10]   Ed Stetzer, "List of Pastor's Retreats and Getaways," https://www.christianitytoday.com/edstetzer/2014/march/free-or-discounted-getaways-for-pastors.html.

Fourth, pray and share with others. Often in life, we have not because we ask not (James 4:3). If you want to be able to take your family to the beach but don't have the money, then ask God to provide. Then, be open to sharing your desire with people. This was our story. My wife loves the beach, and I wanted to take her. We had zero funds and no opportunities; so, we asked God to provide a way. The month before our sabbatical, I officiated at a wedding and got into a conversation with a guest about our sabbatical. He asked what we were doing for it, and I told him — adding we'd love to go to the beach and are praying the Lord would provide. Next thing I knew, we were heading to his condo for two weeks. Friends, God loves us. Ask your good Father to provide the sabbatical experiences you want, trust him and don't be hesitant to talk with others about your desires.

7. Rethink — How will your sabbatical promote a new lifestyle?

Refreshment brings new perspectives. Toward the end of your sabbatical, it's wise to carve out some time to reflect on life and ministry. Notice I did not say at the beginning of your sabbatical. Let refreshment do its work of clearing the fog before you try to see the path. Some types of reflection questions could be:

- What are my top five feelings surrounding ministry right now? Surrounding family? Surrounding my relationship with Jesus?
- Where do I feel the most stress in ministry? In the home? In my relationships?
- What things do I love about my life?

- What things would I change?
- Where is God calling me to courage and sacrifice?
- Where is God inviting me to joyful service?

I would encourage you to write down your reflections. They will become a valuable resource to you later for re-engaging with work as well as communicating to your church the benefits you received from your sabbatical. (See Appendix 4 for an example of a sabbatical proposal.)

A Church-Wide Sending

Your leadership has a written policy, your proposed plan has been approved, and now you are just a couple of months away from showtime. Final preparations are crucial. For a healthy departure, you need to communicate well, delegate and formalize the sending.

Communicate to Your Church

First, communicate about the sabbatical. You have an amazing opportunity to teach your church through this sabbatical. If you are the primary communicator, you may consider preaching some sermons on a theology of work and rest anywhere from six months to a year in advance. This will help prepare your people for your time away. If your church holds member meetings, then start teaching on sabbaticals three to six months in advance. Talk about your personal goals for your sabbatical. Share specific prayer requests. Boast in your weakness and limits, and answer common questions (see Philosophy, "Perceptions of Sabbaticals").

Second, communicate about plurality. Do not miss one of the benefits of a sabbatical (especially for a lead pastor) — it reinforces the plurality of pastors. When the lead guy steps away and other pastors lead in his absence, the clear message is these men are your pastors. Knowing that, we can proactively talk about plurality. The sabbatical gives you the opportunity to imbed two important messages into your church's culture:

1. We love our pastor and want what's best for him and his family.
2. Even though we love our pastor, Jesus' church will go on without him.

The more you can communicate this message before, during and after the sabbatical the better. These concepts erode the all-too-common celebrity-pastor culture in our churches. These ideas reinforce that the pastor is loved but ultimately replaceable. On-going communication from the pastoral team reminds the church to continue praying for their pastor in his absence but also to keep pressing into the work of ministry.

Third, communicate about prayer. What a wonderful opportunity to call your church to pray — for the pastor on sabbatical, for all the leaders filling the gap, for the church to bear fruit, for Jesus to be glorified in this specific season. This call to prayer should begin before the sabbatical and continue throughout its duration.

Delegate and Leave Work

The task of leaving work for several months can be daunting for you and others. You may have heard the old saying, *You can delegate tasks but not responsibility.* The unique thing about a sabbatical is you must delegate both. Delegate tasks to many and responsibility to a few. Decide one or two leaders who will be the go-to people for everyone else on your team, and then dispense your tasks to many leaders. To do this, you must know what you do. Here's a framework for you:[11]

> ***Define*** — Write a list of everything you do. Absolutely everything. After creating the list of everything you do, move onto step two.
>
> ***Eliminate*** — What tasks can wait? What tasks are unnecessary for others to do?
>
> ***Automate*** — Are there any tasks that you can use software or systems to keep you from bogging down your team with unnecessary work?
>
> ***Delegate*** — Everything that remains should be simplified as much as possible and tasked to others (with a written-out process if needed).

First, don't read into the fact I just created the acronym — DEAD. Second, spend adequate time with your delegates, and make sure the one or two team leads who are

---

[11] The eliminate, automate, and delegate framework comes from Timothy Ferriss' *The Four-Hour Workweek* (New York: Harmony, 2007).

responsible have all the need-to-knows. In an ideal world (which we all know ministry is rarely ideal), you'll be able to hand off your tasks and ease into your sabbatical with confidence that all will be covered. But in reality, you will most likely work hard to leave well and still feel unprepared for your sabbatical.

> **Have faith. Leave things as orderly as you can. Trust Jesus. Trust your team.**

That's okay. Have faith. Leave things as orderly as you can. Trust Jesus. Trust your team.

Formalize the Sending

This does not have to be extravagant, but rituals help us process transitions. If a pastor goes off without a word, then he will likely feel under-appreciated and the church will be confused. While praying at a member meeting is great, I would recommend this be church-wide. At the end of the last Sunday morning service before the sabbatical starts, include a time of prayer and sending. Or have a fifteen minute mingle time with snacks after the service. Commemorate the last Sunday before a sabbatical. Again, you can punctuate plurality by having another pastor lead this time. Be sure to express words of encouragement for the pastor who is leaving as well as exhortations to the church.

Encouraging words are important here. Your pastor who has poured out his soul before the Lord on behalf of leading Jesus' church is about to go from sixty to zero in the service department. Questions of worth, value to the congregation and place are going to rise. So, be intentional to use words like:

- "We love you, and we'll miss you."
- "Your absence will be felt, but we're trusting that you will taste and see that the Lord is good."
- "We are going to pray for you today, and we're going to commit as a church to continue to pray for you."

This type of encouragement will help both the church and the pastor going on sabbatical. Some amazing deacons in our church put together a large basket with notes of encouragement, toys for our son and snacks for our road trip. Later, when insecurity threatened to topple me, the fact that we were sent well provided a counter-balance of truth.

Now that we've done a lot of work to prepare, it's time to go on a sabbatical. If you're ready, take a deep breath.

And here we go!

PROCESS (PART 1)

TAKING A SABBATICAL

"Jesus, take the wheel
Take it from my hands
'Cause I can't do this on my own"
– Carrie Underwood

Your alarm screams. The land of the living crashes into your consciousness. Day one of the long-awaited-for and much-planned-for sabbatical starts. Your feet touch down on the floor, and you enter into a whole new world leaving behind the burdens you carried to bed.

Right?

Remember, friends, you are not a machine. There is no off switch that disconnects one part of your life from another. You are a complex, integrated human being and taking a break from ministry is complicated. Now, you can — and should — plan your sabbatical out as much as possible. But you are not the lord of your sabbatical. A good sabbatical is not measured by the execution of your plan. A good sabbatical is experienced as you are present to yourself, others and God's World.

Let me say that again: Your daily task during your sabbatical is to be present.

Being Present with Yourself

Remember the river jar illustrations? As long as the busyness of work keeps us moving, the water stays muddy. When the jar stops shaking, the sediment settles — finally, we see!

I hope you dart out of the gate of your sabbatical with unadulterated joy leaping and laughing into fields of rest. But many of us have underlying thoughts and feelings that work has muddied. Don't be surprised if anxiety, sadness, shame or guilt increase on your sabbatical — often things get worse before they get better. This is normal. The sediment is settling, and Jesus is offering an invitation to be honest with yourself. On the one hand, don't injure yourself more by running away from negative thoughts or feelings. On the other hand, your sabbatical is not the time to beat yourself up or feel bad about feeling bad. In these moments (truly in all moments), Jesus dispenses oceans of compassion and an eternity's worth of patience for us. We cross a line when we are less compassionate and less patient with ourselves than Jesus.

When your inner critic comes out to play on your sabbatical, it's helpful to remember that "whenever our heart condemns us, God is greater than our heart, and he knows everything" (1 John 3:20). While you may be surprised by your inner dialogue occurring on your sabbatical, God is not.

Don't avoid but pay attention to those thoughts and feelings. And then, cast all those cares on Jesus because he cares for you more than you could ever know (1 Peter 5:7).

Henri Nouwen well described our extremes in relation to our inner pain:

> There is a deep hole in your being, like an abyss. You will never succeed in filling that hole, because your needs are inexhaustible. You have to work around it so that gradually the abyss closes ... There are two extremes to avoid: being completely absorbed in your pain and being distracted by so many things that you stay far away from the wound you want to heal.[1]

How do we walk around our abyss on our sabbatical without turning to despair or denial?

I believe the apostle Paul gives us at least a starting point — be "sorrowful yet always rejoicing" (2 Corinthians 6:20). Put another way: we must grieve and delight on our sabbaticals (see "Being Present in God's World" below on delighting).

I hope I'm not projecting my own sabbatical experience on you at this point, but I'm convinced few people know how to grieve well. You may not classify your experiences in ministry as worthy of grieving. But the reality is we experience losses every day, and those losses add up. Dan Allender says this much in his book *To Be Told:*

---

[1] Henri Nouwen, *The Inner Voice of Love: A Journey Through Anguish to Freedom* (New York: Doubleday, 1996), 3.

Even when tragedy has nothing to do with physical death, it still involves a form of death in the shattering of *shalom*, or harmony. A divorce is a death. Sexual abuse is a death. Betrayal in a relationships, the loss of a job, conflict in a marriage, an auto accident, an illness, loss of meaning or hope or joy — are all forms of death. In the Bible God makes it clear that rebellion results in death. Death lies at the heart of all tragedy and at the core of every personal narrative.[2]

To contextualize for us in ministry, the unfounded critique is a death. The member moving on to another church is a death. The member leaving the faith is a death. The painful conflict in your leadership team as well as a thousand other difficulties are deaths.

Friends, the losses you refuse to own will ultimately own you.[3] Every breathing person is trying to make sense of his or her story. Being present to yourself in your sabbatical is taking advantage of the opportunity to process difficulties. If certain situations or people come to mind

The losses you refuse to own will ultimately own you.

again and again no matter what you do, then ask the Lord why you can't shake the thoughts.

This is the dreaded struggle of a sabbatical. Sabbaticals are the long-awaited opportunity to rest, yet entering into rest can be sabotaged by your own heart and mind. How do you

---

[2] Dan Allender, *To Be Told* (Colorado Springs: WaterBrook Press, 2005), 16–17.

[3] Rich Plass made this statement in a teaching session I attended in 2011.

turn off the replaying and revisiting of work, conflict and stress? Simply put — ask the Lord to search and know your anxious thoughts (Psalm 139:23).

First, ask Jesus to reveal opportunities in our thought-life. We get so riled up at the fact that we can't turn off certain thoughts, when maybe the thought is there because God wants us to engage it. This engagement must happen in relation to Jesus through prayer. Your anxious thoughts are an opportunity to either run away, fall in or run to Jesus. Talk to him. Ask him why this thought keeps coming to mind. Ask him what he wants to teach you, or what he wants you to do with the thought. Turn the consternation into a conversation and find meaningful communion with your Savior.

Second, ask Jesus to reveal misplaced worship. What we worship shapes our thoughts and feelings. If we are miserable because we cannot stop thinking about a crisis or keep replaying a conversation or dread a future conversation, then maybe we have a worship problem. Hannah Anderson in her book *Humble Roots* says it well,

> Humility teaches us to trust God. And suddenly a burden rolls off our back. We are no longer responsible to produce faith in another person's heart. (As if we ever could.) We are no longer responsible for someone's relationship with Christ. We are no longer responsible for the Holy Spirit's work. He is.[4]

---

[4] Hannah Anderson, *Humble Roots: How Humility Grounds and Nourishes Your Soul* (Chicago: Moody Press, 2016), 113.

Perhaps some of our inner unrest on a sabbatical is not evidence of how much we care for others but an indicator that we've tried to play God. Sometimes the easiest way to settle the swirling stress is to surrender control and entrust the souls of others to Jesus.

Third, ask Jesus to reveal losses we need to grieve. Jesus may be bringing painful events to mind because you need to grieve, forgive and move on. While everyone processes grief in their own way, studies show that telling your story is a powerful tool for healing from traumatic experiences.[5] Neuropsychiatrist Daniel Siegel and parenting expert Tina Bryson write, "The drive to understand why things happen to us is so strong that the brain will continue to try making sense of an experience until it succeeds . . . we can help this process along through storytelling."[6]

Here are two storytelling options for your sabbatical. *First, write out your story.* If you're not ready to talk with anyone, journal. Write your painful experiences as if you're talking to Jesus. Write out the details of the event. Name the primary emotion you felt. And detail the interpretations you made — about yourself, others and God.[7] Putting ink to page can be a

---

[5]   Deborah   Serani,   "Why   Your   Story   Matters," https://www.psychologytoday.com/us/blog/two-takes-depression/ 201401/why-your-story-matters.

[6] Daniel Siegel and Tina Bryson, The Whole-Brain Child: 12 Revolutionary Strategies to Nurture Your Child's Developing Mind, (New York: Bantam Books Trade Paperbacks, 2012), 29.

[7] This process for understanding your story was taken from Rich Plass and Jim Cofield's *The Relational Soul* (Downers Grove: IVP Books, 2014), 173–77.

tactile expression of casting your cares on the Lord (1 Peter 5:7).

Second, share with a trustworthy friend/family member. You may share after writing out your story or dive into verbal processing. However, it's important for the person you're sharing with to know that the process of sharing is healing in and of itself. God has wired us this way. Your friend doesn't have to be a trained counselor or an expert. Your friend doesn't have to try to

> **It's counterintuitive, but sabbaticals are for grieving. Grief helps us mature.**

fix situations or provide next steps. The point is for you to have a safe space to share openly and honestly so that Jesus can bring you to a place of understanding and grieving for what you've lived.

It's counterintuitive, but sabbaticals are for grieving. Grief helps us mature. Part of maturity is learning how to hold both sorrow and joy in open hands before Jesus. This kind of heavy lifting takes time. And being present to ourselves can create tension when also seeking to be present with others. Let's tackle the tension head on.

Being Present to Others

Planning and agreeing to both times of solitude and connection with others can go a long way toward a smooth sabbatical. If you are married and/or have children, your sabbatical will be a shared experience. And a shared experience means multiplied expectations. The more expectations brought into a sabbatical, the more complexity increases.

First, communicate expectations. Hopefully, your plan includes goals for your marriage and family. Beyond that, it's wise to talk with each family member about what they hope to get out of the sabbatical. It's equally important for you to share your hopes and dreams. This brings up the reality that you take a break from your job, but you do not take a break from all work. A sabbatical is not a break from loving your neighbor as yourself. You just reallocate your labor. Listen to what your wife and children desire. Love them. Be present when you're with them. And remember that it's better to give than to receive — even on your sabbatical (Acts 20:35).

Second, be gracious with one another. In the same way that negative thoughts and feelings can surprise you on a sabbatical, relational tensions can too. This makes sense. When working, relational patterns can go unaddressed. When spending more time with others, the friction becomes harder to ignore. Relational problems may feel like a distraction to sabbatical refreshment, but it's actually an invitation from God to greater intimacy and refreshment.

Don't be shocked when you fail to meet each other's expectations, and plan to extend grace to one another. There were several times on my sabbatical when I needed to pull away from family time for a few minutes to pray. There were other times when I needed to play with our son to provide space for my wife to get alone. Discerning between solitude and relationship as well as serving and being served takes wisdom. Be gracious with one another and humble before the Lord as you figure out new rhythms.

Third, be flexible with your expectations. Often what we hope for is not what we need. We get into trouble when we cling to our expectations. In his little book *Life Together*, Dietrich Bonhoeffer makes a profound statement about community that — if you will permit me some freedom to substitute the word "community" for "rest" — reveals a profound truth about rest too.

> He who loves his dream of (rest) more than the (rest) itself becomes a destroyer of the latter, even though his personal intentions may be ever so honest and earnest and sacrificial. God hates visionary dreaming; it makes the dreamer proud and pretentious. The man who fashions a visionary ideal of (rest) demands that it be realized by God, by others, and by himself.[8]

Friends, we plan for rest, but the Lord gives true rest. We may think rest comes from reclining on a beach, but maybe Jesus wants to give true rest through resolving conflict with our wife or through shepherding our children through disobedience. A sabbatical is most meaningful when we humble ourselves to follow Jesus' leading into rest — especially when our relationships don't follow our plan or feel restful in the moment.

Too often, our imagination of the good life is people leaving us alone while we do what we want when we want. It's almost as if we imagine ourselves on a throne in heaven

---

[8] Dietrich Bonhoeffer, *Life Together: A Discussion of Christian Fellowship* (New York: Harper & Row, 1954), 27.

above and unaffected by all the troubles of life. If that's our expectation for a sabbatical, then we're in for trouble.

How amazing that Jesus — who was on that throne above it all — decided to come down. He became a man. He submitted himself to trouble, conflict, pain and death *so that* he could give us life. Pastor, we have been shown such amazing grace; let's show that same grace to our families on our sabbatical.

Being Present in God's World

For the first week or two, the impulse to check email or think about work will be strong. Letting go of knowing what's going on and killing off thoughts of work will require an active faith in Jesus and those leading in your absence. Abstaining from work and entering rest is a process.

Give it time.

More contemplative pastors describe this experience as moving from doing to being. However, if many of us are honest, these types of statements around rest can be confusing and frustrating. I remember talking with an older pastor who coached me to have an extended day of silence and solitude. I asked, "What do I do for five hours?" His response, "Don't focus on doing; focus on being."

Don't focus on doing; focus on being.

Thanks, Yoda.

At that point in my life, I didn't get it. Over the years, I have grown in my understanding of what that wise pastor meant. But I have also come to see that the Bible gives us clearer instruction than, "Don't do; just be." Being present is an activity that is achieved in the practice of delighting. Delight forces us to rearrange our activity toward an experience that requires lingering, patience and stillness. This can feel like inactivity, but we nonetheless lean into a moment when we delight. Consider how David puts all these ideas of seeking, dwelling and delighting together:

> One thing have I asked of the LORD,
>   that will I seek after:
> that I may dwell in the house of the LORD
>   all the days of my life,
> to gaze upon the beauty of the LORD
>   and to inquire in his temple. (Psalm 27:4)

Notice the verbs. Asking and seeking are words of intense activity. Far from passive imagery, David imports visions of hot pursuit into our imagination. But notice the next verb — dwell. Intense pursuit is manifest in the experience of inhabiting the space of God's presence. We realize David's intense activity is geared toward a goal of *being with the Lord*. The two final verbs bring it all together — to gaze and inquire. The word "inquire" is actually the same Hebrew word "seek" that we see at first. The search for being in the Lord's presence is obtained through *gazing upon the Lord's beauty*. Isn't that just another way of saying to delight in the Lord?[9]

---

[9] In fact, this is why the NLT translates this verse, "delighting in the LORD's perfections and meditating in his Temple."

Being present on your sabbatical looks like paying attention to the painful parts of your life, but it also resembles an earnest pursuit of enjoyment.

Presence comes through delighting in God and his world. Think about how refreshed you feel after experiencing an amazing evening with friends or savoring an incredible meal or soaking in the sun on a gorgeous day. This idea of delight takes us back to the notion of sabbaticals as an extended sabbath. We sabbath and sabbatical to enjoy God and the good gifts he gives. Like God on the seventh day, we take an extended break from our work to step back and enjoy the goodness of the world we live in.

Now don't be fooled — delight takes time. Delight demands we slow down. Delight requires patience and cultivation. It's not instant but a process. Enjoying God and the gifts he gives is how you move from a frantic search for identity in what you do to a grounded experience of being a child in his presence. Enjoyment requires faith to trust that God is a good Father who gives good gifts to his children (Matthew 7:11). Enjoyment creates a deep well of gratitude that just might change your whole outlook on life.

Pastor, on your sabbatical Jesus gives you permission to step back from your work and enjoy him, others and the good gifts of his world. You don't have to wallow in guilt because Jesus died for your guilt. You don't have to feel ashamed thinking, *I don't deserve a sabbatical* because your Father always gives underserved gifts.

There's nothing to earn here, and all you must do is enjoy your sabbatical *as a gift of grace.*

Go on! Open that present and smile like you are a five-year old.

My prayer for you is that grace becomes more real on your sabbatical. My sabbatical was the first time in my life where I didn't feel pressure to be or do something. It was a life-changing experience of the gospel — that I am loved by God apart from what I do. That experience was transformative.

May God do this and more for you.

Finally, let me encourage you to get outside as much as possible. My family and I decided to take a fifteen-day road trip to camp in the Black Hills National Forest, Yellowstone and Rocky Mountains National Park. I wanted (and I think even needed) to get to big sky country and to mountains that leave a lasting impression on the skyline.

Beholding beauty takes effort but pays off.

John Piper once described how he fought lust in his younger years, and his description helps us when considering how to delight in God's world:

> I remember as I struggled with these things in my teenage years and in my college years — I knew how I could fight most effectively in those days. And I've developed other strategies over the years that have proved very effective. And one way of fighting was simply to get out of the dark places, get out of the lonely rooms, get out of the boxed-in places, get out of the places where it's just small me and my mind and what I

can do with it, and get out where I am just surrounded by color and beauty and bigness and loveliness.[10]

Pastor, don't spend your sabbatical cooped up in small spaces. Get out into the open places and allow staggering beauty to confront your soul. Let that beauty refresh you in the beauty of God. Be reminded on your sabbatical that what you do is important and your work is not in vain (1 Corinthians 15:58), but your ministry is not at the center of the universe. Embrace that you are not essential to Jesus' church marching on but are nonetheless loved and valued for the part you play.

Embrace that you are not essential to Jesus' church marching on but are nonetheless loved and valued for the part you play.

---

[10] John Piper, "Do you see the Joy of God in the Sun? Part 2," https://www.desiringgod.org/messages/do-you-see-the-joy-of-god-in-the-sun-part-2#/listen/excerpt.

PROCESS (PART 2)

RETURNING FROM A SABBATICAL

"But I still haven't found
What I'm looking for"

– U2

A sabbatical can be an incredible gift from Jesus, but it cannot take his place. Even the best of sabbaticals will leave you wanting in some way, and that's okay. You weren't looking to your sabbatical to make you whole; you took a break from ministry before ministry broke you. Now it's time to get back to work.

What does healthy reintegration into work and ongoing retreat into rest look like from here?

Reintegration into Work

The last week of my sabbatical was the hardest for me. Anxiety and insecurity were at a record high. Here are a couple steps that helped me.

First, create realistic expectations for yourself. However long you are away, expect it to take the same amount of time to feel settled back into work. For example, if you were gone for three months, then wrap your mind around a three-month reintegration period. Maybe you'll be storming the castle in less time, but frustration abounds for the unrealistic. You were gone a long time. Be patient with yourself and others you work alongside.

A great way to shoot your sabbatical tranquility in the face is to be led by the tyranny of the urgent. Getting caught up on three months of church life will feel urgent. Start by meeting with your key leaders and take it a day at a time. Remember you are a human, not a machine. Wade in, pray a bunch and enjoy the process.

Second, communicate, communicate, communicate. Expressing gratitude often and in many contexts is essential. You just received a gift that others paid for with their sacrificial service. Saying thank you in multiple settings and in a multitude of ways displays that you see their sacrifice. While you may be tempted to come back with critique for decisions or actions of certain leaders, it's important to encourage your team — lest bitterness take hold. Hopefully as a result of others doing your job, they have a greater appreciation for you and you for them. Make your thankfulness known.

Also, share specific details of your sabbatical experience and takeaways with your elder team. Allow the team to speak into where, when and what would be good to share with the church. As you share with your elders, do your best to be prepared. You want a clear articulation of the benefits of your sabbatical. A haphazard, rambling share-session does not inspire confidence in the legitimacy of sabbaticals — or their hard work.

Finally, ask lots of questions to hear from your leaders and members. By asking questions, you get to hear the benefits the church experienced while you were gone. For us, our church realized they don't need me but enjoy having me around. That's a win! I wanted to highlight to the church not only the benefits my family received but also articulate for the church the benefits they experienced through our sabbatical. Listening well and forming words for their experience can be a special gift to the church.

Third, celebrate all Jesus has done. In personal conversations and together as a congregation, celebrate the experience. Sabbaticals are a counter-intuitive, upside-down Kingdom expression. They are a taste-and-see moment of grace. Like all experiences of grace, you must celebrate it and the people who made it possible. Celebration will help with your transition back, but it will also instill a culture in your church where folks value work and rest alike as means to glorify and honor King Jesus.

Retreat into Rest

One of the greatest benefits of a sabbatical is the clarification revealed around work-rest rhythms. The clarity I received on my sabbatical was painful but sweet. I had to accept that I had been fooling myself. Pre-sabbatical, I worked hard to prepare gospel feasts for everyone else, yet I tried to live off the crumbs that fell from the table. My time away helped me re-envision my life. If you don't address and change unhealthy rest habits after a sabbatical, then you won't make it to your next one.

In addition, some pastors are unable to take a sabbatical because their church can't afford for them to be gone for three months — while other pastors won't take a sabbatical because they are too afraid to ask for one and still other pastors know their church culture would punish them for asking for rest. As pastors, we must be honest with our reasons for not taking a sabbatical. But is there any hope for the pastor who can't take three months off? I believe so because you can still implement healthy rhythms of rest.

Here are four spaces for rest to evaluate and make adjustments.

First, daily rest — are you daily abiding in Christ? Before my sabbatical, I didn't feel like I had the freedom to sit alone for even fifteen minutes a day. That was a big problem. Consider the amount of time you need with Jesus a day to be healthy, and make it happen. This time should involve stillness, God's Word, solitude, and prayer. Maybe you journal for a few minutes, go on a slow walk, sit on a bench and stare at a tree while you reflect on God's Word. Find your own way, but don't fool yourself. Rest daily in your relationship with Jesus. Something or someone will always beg for your attention. However, this daily feasting on the bread of life will make you a more loving and patient pastor, husband, father, and friend.

Second, weekly rest — are you practicing a weekly Sabbath? The most life-changing aspect of my sabbatical was it taught me how to sabbath. Pete Scazzero says that a sabbath is a break from paid and unpaid work.[1] After reading that sentence, I realized I had never taken a true day of rest in my life. Our days off were always filled with some type of work that I disliked and dreaded. But a Sabbath is for delight in God and his gifts.

> **There are six days a week for sorrow; our sabbath is a day to display faith by choosing joy.**

It's a day to put off the heaviness of life and to choose joy. If you are like me, that last sentence might strike you as disingenuous. How can you choose joy when life is hard? Isn't it unhealthy to ignore sorrow? Well, the Bible commands us to, "Rejoice in the Lord always; again I will say, rejoice" (Philippians 4:4). No matter what is going on, rejoice. As we say around our house, there are six days a week for sorrow; our sabbath is a day to display faith by choosing joy.[2]

---

[1] "Once we stop, we accept God's invitation to rest. God rested after his work of creation. Every seventh day, we are to do the same (Genesis 2:1–4). We engage in activities that restore and replenish us — from napping, hiking, reading, and eating good food to enjoying hobbies and playing sports. The key is to rest from both paid and unpaid work." Scazzero, *Emotionally Healthy Leader,* 147.

[2] John Mark Comer, *Garden City*, 225. "Jews have been practicing the art of Sabbath for millennia. We have a lot we can learn from them. They talk a lot about menuha — another Hebrew word that's translated 'rest,' but it's a very specific kind of rest. It's not just a nap on the couch. It's a restfulness that's also a celebration. It's often translated 'happiness.' And to the Jews, menuha is something you create. It's not just that you stop working and sit on the couch for a day every week. It's about cultivating an environment, an atmosphere to enjoy your life, your world, and your God.

When we set apart a regular day to enjoy life, then life becomes more enjoyable. It's not rocket science, but I lived my whole life missing this. God loves us so much that he tells us to stop once a week and enjoy. What a kind Father!

So how do you plan your sabbath day?

Ask yourself these two questions: 1) Is it worship?, and 2) Is it refreshing?[3] These questions are guardrails to keep us cruising down the boulevard of our day of rest. Learning how to sabbath is a process. We try and fail. But if we keep trying, we find a rhythm in life that reminds us we are not defined by our work but by the love of Jesus.

Third, regular retreats — are you getting away for solitude? With some planning, there is no reason you can't get away three or four times a year for a day or an overnight retreat. Getting out of town for a day or two can reinvigorate your passion for Jesus and vision for his church. If married with kids, love your wife by watching the kids on a Saturday or weekend so she can have some precious solitude.

On these retreats, you choose alternative activities from normal ministry. You trade interacting with others for solitude with Jesus. You stop talking on behalf of God in order to listen to God. In doing so, you are following the pattern and practice of Jesus who regularly got away (Mark 1:35–36; 6:46; Luke 5:16; 6:12; John 6:15). What you do is not

---

It's more of a mode of being than a twenty-four-hour time slot . . . It isn't a day to be sad. Because the Sabbath is a day for menuha — for the celebration of life in God's very good world."

³ These two questions are adapted from John Mark Comer's questions: "Is this worship? Is this rest?" *Garden City,* 192. For many, we can more instinctively answer what's refreshing before naming what brings us rest.

as important as creating a special space to connect with and hear from God. Days like this can feel like a waste in our pragmatic culture. But remember we are governed by a different culture — God's Kingdom — where solitude provides soul-satisfying benefits. (Check out Appendix 5 for How to Take a Personal Retreat.)

Fourth, yearly vacations — are you taking vacation time? Your vacation can be a mini-sabbatical. You don't have to check your email or take a break from spending time with Jesus. It's not an opportunity for escaping from work into the isolation of exaggerated play with no time spent in reflection. You can incorporate

Take advantage of your time off — no one else is going to take it for you.

the same practices from Chapter 3 on a micro-level into your vacation. In this way, every year offers you something to look forward to — a little sabbatical.

Friends, don't waste away while leaving valuable nutrients on the table. Take advantage of your time off — no one else is going to take it for you.

CONCLUSION

Thanks for hanging with me until the end. I promise this will be quick.

I hope and pray that you are more willing to take a break from ministry before ministry breaks you — not because we find ministry lacking as a worthy endeavor. We agree with the apostle Paul when he said, "I will most gladly spend and be spent for your souls" (2 Corinthians 12:15). But we also recognize that man does not live by work alone. There is something askew in us if we can't stop working. Rest forces us to deal with the realities of our pride, insecurity and sometimes idolatry. On the other hand, we realize we can idolize rest too. We can look to a vacation or a sabbatical to save us from the parts of our lives and ourselves that we don't like. Work and rest are great gifts but terrible saviors.

Jesus is the Savior of the world. He's your Savior too. May you walk in wisdom with the help of the Spirit and with your community of believers. May you be the kind of pastor who works alongside and rests with Jesus for your good, for the goodness of your neighbor and for the ultimate aim of God's glory.

See — I told you it would be quick.

PRACTICES

APPENDICES

APPENDIX ONE

SABBATICAL POLICY EXAMPLES

Example 1 — Apostles Church Sabbatical Policy

Apostles Church Uptown seeks to care for the long-term spiritual and emotional health of our employees and their families by providing a Sabbatical Leave.

Sabbatical Leave is 12 consecutive weeks of paid time off every 5th year for full-time pastors and 5 consecutive weeks of paid time off every 7th year for non-pastoral full-time staff. Compensation shall be equivalent to the employee's full salary for the sabbatical period granted and all related benefits shall continue during the sabbatical period. All expenses related to the sabbatical activities will be at the sole cost of the employee. Additional compensation, bonus or financial allowance, may be granted to the employee during for their sabbatical upon elder discretion.

The employee may take Sabbatical Leave at any time during their sabbatical year, but the requested dates must be submitted to the elders for approval along with the completed Sabbatical Leave Form no later than the first day of the fiscal year (July 1st) in which they plan to take their leave. During a Sabbatical Leave, the employee will receive their regularly allotted Holidays and Flex Days plus 5 Vacation Days (not to be taken consecutively to Sabbatical Leave).

Example 2 — Sojourn Community Church Sabbatical Policy

Sojourn Community Church's full-time pastoral staff will be eligible for a 6-month sabbatical leave upon completion of 7 years of employment by Sojourn and in subsequent 7-year service periods thereafter.

Purpose

- The purpose of the sabbatical is to provide the pastor time for spiritual reflection and refreshment, personal study, and development of skills, or to provide the pastor a time to research, write, or devote himself to a specified project related to his ministry area.

Requirements

- The Pastor must have completed at least 7 years of pastoral employment with Sojourn Community Church.
- Pastors intending on taking sabbatical leave must submit a proposed sabbatical plan in writing to the Council of Elders for approval at least 6 months prior to the intended sabbatical. The Council of

Elders will review the plan, offer suggestions or modifications if indicated, and then approve the plan. *Note: The Council of Elders maintain the authority to reject or postpone a sabbatical plan based on the appropriateness of the plan, number of pastors requesting leave at the same time, or the Church's capacity to fulfill the Pastor's ministry responsibilities during the leave.*

- The Pastor must commit to 1 year of service to the church directly following the Sabbatical leave.
- The Pastor must provide a written testimonial to the Council of Elders within a reasonable time frame following the Sabbatical leave indicating the details of any spiritual insight/wisdom/growth gained; or any research, writing, and ministry-related work completed.

Compensation

- During the Sabbatical leave, the Pastor will retain his contracted compensation arrangement with Sojourn Community Church. Pastors are encouraged to pursue grant funding and/or outside support for their related expenses.

Additional Considerations

- Eligible Pastors may elect to take 6 months of sabbatical leave over the course of 2 years following their 7ᵗʰ year of employment by Sojourn Community Church (i.e. 3 months in the first year, 3 months in the second year).

- During the year of the sabbatical leave, the Pastor's normal vacation benefit will be reduced to 1 week. *Note: If the pastor elects to take a sabbatical over the course of 2 years as mentioned above, the vacation benefit will be reduced by half in each year in which the 3-month leave is taken.*

APPENDIX TWO

RECOMMENDED READING FOR PERSONAL SOUL CARE AND REFRESHMENT

To Be Told: God Invites You to Coauthor Your Future by Dan Allender

Leading with a Limp: Take Full Advantage of Your Most Powerful Weakness by Dan Allender

Humble Roots: How Humility Grounds and Nourishes the Soul by Hannah Anderson

Invitation to Solitude and Silence: Experiencing God's Transforming Presence by Ruth Haley Barton

Strengthening the Soul of Your Leadership: Seeking God in the Crucible of Ministry by Ruth Haley Barton

Surrender to Love: Discovering the Heart of Christian Spirituality by David Benner

A Timbered Choir: The Sabbath Poems 1979-1997 by Wendell Berry

You Can Change: God's Transforming Power over Our Sinful Behavior and Negative Emotions by Tim Chester

Leading on Empty: Refilling Your Tank and Renewing Your Passion by Wayne Cordeiro

Recapturing the Wonder: Transcendent Faith in a Disenchanted World by Mike Cosper

Strong and Weak: Embracing a Life Love, Risk and True Flourishing by Andy Crouch

Imperfect Pastor: Discovering Joy in our Limitations through a Daily Apprenticeship with Jesus by Zack Eswine

Spurgeon's Sorrows: Realistic Hope for those who Suffer from Depression by Zack Eswine

The Freedom of Self-Forgetfulness: The Path of True Christian Joy by Tim Keller

A Grief Observed by C. S. Lewis

Humility: True Greatness by C.J. Mahaney

Abba's Child: The Cry of the Heart for Intimate Belonging by Brennan Manning

Free of Me: Why Life Is Better When It's Not About You by Sharon Miller

Reset: Living a Grace-Paced Life in a Burnout Culture by David Murray

The Inner Voice of Love: A Journey through Anguish to Freedom by Henri Nouwen

Reaching Out: The Three Movements of the Spiritual Life by Henri Nouwen

The Contemplative Pastor: Returning to the Art of Spiritual Direction by Eugene Peterson

The Relational Soul: Moving from False Self to Deep Connection by Rich Plass and Jim Cofield

Emotionally Healthy Leader: How Transforming Your Inner Life Will Deeply Transform Your Church, Team, and the World by Peter Scazzero

Lincoln's Melancholy: How Depression Challenged a President and Fueled His Greatness by Joshua Shenk

When People Are Big and God Is Small: Overcoming Peer Pressure, Codependency, and the Fear of Man by Ed Welch

Redemption: Freed by Jesus from the Idols We Worship and the Wounds We Carry by Mike Wilkerson

APPENDIX THREE

HOW TO JOURNAL

Journaling is good for you. But how do you do it? Here are some thoughts:

1st — Keep it Simple and Consistent

I find folks do not journal because they feel like they need to have something profound to say or need to write a novella every day. Focus on consistency over content. Three sentences a day for a decade is more helpful than thirty sentences every two months.

2nd — Keep it Honest

Don't fall into the trap of wondering who will read your journal. Ask God to help you be honest. Make your journal a conversation with Jesus and tell him what's going on.

3rd — Keep it Holistic

Focus on what's at the forefront of your mind, but also be sure to include all aspects of your life at some point. You can do this by rotating one or two of the following questions each day:

- What have I experienced in the past 24 hours?
- What emotions am I feeling?
- What am I thinking about God, myself or others in light of what I've experienced?
- What do I need to celebrate and give thanks to God?
- What do I need to mourn and let go?
- What is making me anxious, angry or sad and why?
- What is God calling me to do today?
- Is there anyone I need to forgive or ask for forgiveness?

Journaling can be a great and revelatory gift for you. Even though I just gave you prompting questions, journaling is what you make it. Find your way, friends, and enjoy the process.

APPENDIX FOUR

SABBATICAL PROPOSAL EXAMPLE

Overview

The purpose of my sabbatical will be for refreshment and will be 12 weeks starting June 1 through August 24.

Sabbatical Goals

1. To grow in my love for Jesus and his Word.
2. To create special memories with my family.
3. To work through my impatient responses to my wife and kids.

Sabbatical Plan

1. Reorder — *How Will Your Schedule Promote Refreshment?*

What I will say no to — Fasting

- Social media
- Emails
- Draining home projects
- Attending my own church

What I will say yes to — Feasting

- Lingering in the scriptures
- Praying with family
- Going to bed early
- Prioritizing time spent with family over getting stuff done
- Attending another church
- Organizing a weekly date night with my wife
- Planning a weekly feast with my family to celebrate God's goodness and love

2. Revive — *How Will Your Soul Care Promote Refreshment?*

- I will spend at least an hour with Jesus every day.
- I will read through Proverbs twice and study Philippians in depth with Gordon Fee's commentary.

- Personally, I will read and journal through *Humble Roots: How Humility Grounds and Nourished the Soul* by Hannah Anderson and *Reset: Living a Grace-Paced Life in a Burnout Culture* by David Murray.
- My wife will read through *Emotionally Healthy Spirituality* by Pete Scazzero.
- I will spend a day a week in extended prayer (at least an hour).

3. Rejuvenate — How Will Your Health Promote Refreshment?

- Twice a week I will go on long walks (at least a mile).
- Twice a week I will lift weights.
- Besides our feast, I will count calories.
- I will get 8 hours of sleep a night.

4. Recreate — How Will Fun Promote Refreshment?

- Weeks 1–4 we will travel to camp in Colorado.
- Weeks 5–8 we will stay home.
- Week 9 my wife and I will travel without the kids to stay in Destin, Florida.
- Weeks 10–12 we will stay home.
- My son and I will try out geocaching together.
- I will read the Harry Potter series.
- My wife and I will catch up on movies we've wanted to see.

5. Reconnect — How Will Your Relationships Promote Refreshment?

- Daily meals with immediate family and daily 1:1 conversation with my wife.
- Once a week 1:1 time with each child.
- We will see extended family for a couple days while dropping off the kids for our Destin trip.
- I will grab lunch/dinner with my elder team once a month for friendship time.
- I will go fly fishing with John at least once.
- I will grab a phone call with my friend, Bill, once a month to discuss how the sabbatical is going.

6. Refinance — How Will Your Money Promote Refreshment?

- Books purchased by church
- Destin lodging is funded by non-profit
- $100 for gas round trip (used online gas calculator)
- $150 for groceries for two
- $200 for eating out
- **$450 total for Destin trip taken out of sabbatical savings**
- We already own all our camping gear for our family Colorado trip
- $200 for campsites
- $300 for gas (used online gas calculator)
- $500 for groceries for four weeks
- $600 for eating out

- $300 for adventure opportunities like putt-putt or water parks
- **$1,900 for total trip taken out of sabbatical savings**

7. Rethink — How Will Your Sabbatical Promote a New Lifestyle?

- I will get away for solitude for an 8-hour period for two days during the last two weeks of my sabbatical for rethinking and reflecting on life and ministry.
- I will reflect on Psalm 127 during these times.
- I will answer the questions provided in the Sojourn Network *Sabbaticals* book (pp.41-42; 82) and work toward goals for healthier rhythms in my scheduling.

APPENDIX FIVE

HOW TO TAKE A PERSONAL RETREAT

The following suggestions are by no means exhaustive, but I hope they stir your imagination to give you the gumption to schedule this life-giving experience soon.

Ideas for a personal retreat (in no particular order):

- All you need is a Bible, a pad of paper, and a pen.
- Choose a Psalm for the year that you sit with, pray through and journal about every retreat.
- Read through a specific book of the Bible out loud from start to finish.
- Go on prayer walks.
- Pray and journal through pain points in your life.
- Set a timer and sit still in silence praying about whatever comes to mind.
- Sing songs of worship.
- Stare at a tree, pay attention to yourself and surroundings and talk to God about whatever you are noticing.

- Memorize a verse or two and then mull over those verses all day.
- Process what has happened in life since your last retreat.
- Ask God for a vision for the next season of life.
- Ask the Spirit to reveal brokenness and sin so that you can confess your weaknesses and sins.
- Ask the Spirit to highlight evidence of grace in your life so you can celebrate.
- Rehearse the gospel story to yourself. Remember the love that God has for you in Christ.

Select two to four of these options and get out of town with Jesus for four hours, a day or a weekend trip. This space is not about performance or retreating the "right" way. It's a sacred space to be alone with Jesus and to allow him to do what only he can — give your soul rest.

ACKNOWLEDGMENTS

To the Sojourn Network, thank you for creating the space for friendships that by God's grace will help me go the long haul in ministry. I wrote this book with you — my fellow Sojourn Network pastors — in mind, and I pray that we can complete the race God has given us together.

To Dave Harvey and Ronnie Martin, thank you for your ongoing support to just keep writing. Your encouragement has fanned the flame of this calling for me, and I am eternally grateful. Thank you for entrusting this weighty and joyful project to me. It's been an honor. And a big thank you to Ronnie and Casey Smith for your enthusiasm and editorial prowess. I've loved collaborating with you two.

To the elders and staff at Sojourn in Chattanooga (Jeremy Lucarelli, Marc Loizeaux, Michael Meredith, Alex Baxley and Lauren Brett), thank you for supporting me in such a way that I had time to write this book in the midst of full-time ministry. It is a joy to serve Jesus alongside you leaders (as well as all of our other deacons and volunteers). You are an amazing group of people. Sojourn is better with you, and I am better because of you too.

To my dudes who chat with me once a month, thank you Rob Maine, Dave Owens and Chris Fowler for your friendship and love. Sharing life with you three men has become one of God's surprising means of grace in my life.

To my family, I love going to work every day, but I love coming home more. Rachel, your love, support, and friendship keep me going. You are the most amazing person I know, and I am so grateful that we belong to each other. I love you. Justus and Haven, being present with you at the end of the day fills my heart with joy. You are a gift to me, and I love you.

To Jesus, thank you for life, freedom and the ability to serve alongside you through your Spirit. Thank you that you've promised never to leave us or forsake us in ministry or any other part of our lives. May this book honor you and help us all be closer to you.

If you're interested in sabbatical coaching, I'd love to chat. Please email me at rusty@sojournchattanooga.com.

ABOUT THE AUTHOR

Rusty McKie serves as the lead pastor of Sojourn Community Church in Chattanooga, Tennessee. He has contributed articles for thegospelcoalition.com, AmICalled.com, and sojournnetwork.com. He has been married to Rachel for thirteen years, and they have two dearly loved children.

Rusty loves working and resting alongside family and friends in his beautiful city, Chattanooga. Connect with him on Facebook and Twitter.

ABOUT SOJOURN NETWORK

Throughout the pages of the New Testament, and especially in the book of Acts, we observe a pattern: men and women, through prayer and dependence of God and empowered by the Spirit, are sent by God (often through suffering) to spread the Word of the Lord. As this great news of new life in Christ spread into the neighboring cities, regions, provinces, and countries, gatherings of new believers formed into local communities called churches. As these gatherings formed by the thousands in the first century, the early church — taking its cue from the scriptures — raised up qualified, called, and competent men to lead and shepherd these new congregations.

Two-thousand years later, God is still multiplying his gospel in and through his church, and the Good Shepherd is still using pastors to lead and shepherd God's people. In Sojourn Network, we desire to play our part in helping these pastors plant, grow, and multiply healthy churches.

We realize that only the Spirit can stir people's hearts and bring them into community with other believers in Jesus. Yet by offering the pastors in our network a strong vision of planting, growing, and multiplying healthy churches and by providing them with thorough leadership assessment, funding for new churches and staff, coaching, training, renewal, and resources, we can best steward their gifts for the benefit and renewal of their local congregations.

Since 2011, our aim at Sojourn Network has been to provide the care and support necessary for our pastors to lead their churches with strength and joy — and to finish ministry well.

OTHER "HOW-TO" BOOKS

Here are the current books in the "How-To" series. Stay tuned for more.

Healthy Plurality = Durable Church: "How-To" Build and Maintain a Healthy Plurality of Elders by Dave Harvey

Life-Giving-Groups: "How-To" Grow Healthy, Multiplying Community Groups by Jeremy Linneman

Charting the Course: "How-To" Navigate the Legal Side of a Church Plant by Tim Beltz

Redemptive Participation: A "How-To" Guide for Pastors in Culture by Mike Cosper

Filling Blank Spaces: "How-To" Work with Visual Artists in Your Church by Michael Winters

*Before the Lord, Before the Church: "How-To" Plan a Child
Dedication Service* by Jared Kennedy with Megan Kennedy

*Sabbaticals: "How-To" Take a Break from Ministry before Ministry
Breaks You* by Rusty McKie

*Leaders through Relationship: "How-To" Develop Leaders in the Local
Church* by Kevin Galloway

Raising the Dust: "How-To" Equip Deacons to Serve the Church by
Gregg Allison & Ryan Welsh (forthcoming)

Healthy Plurality = Durable Church: "How-To" Build and Maintain a Healthy Plurality of Elders by Dave Harvey

Have you ever wondered what separates a healthy church from an unhealthy church when they have the same doctrine (and even methods) on paper? The long-term health and durability of a church simply cannot exceed the health of her elders who lead, teach, shepherd, and pray the church forward. Therefore, building and maintaining a healthy plurality of elders is the key to durability. Yet a healthy plurality is a delicate thing working through hardship and the difficulties of relationship while pursuing the noble task of eldership. If you wish to grow deeper in your theology of eldership to lead with a healthy, biblical vision of plurality, then this is your "How-To" guide.

Life-Giving-Groups: "How-To" Grow Healthy, Multiplying Community Groups by Jeremy Linneman

Cultivate life-giving, Christ-centered communities. After many years of leading small groups and coaching hundreds of small group leaders, pastor and writer Jeremy Linneman has come to a bold conviction: Community groups are the best place for us — as relational beings — to become mature followers of Christ. This short book seeks to answer two questions: How can our community groups cultivate mature disciples of Christ? And how can our groups grow and multiply to sustain a healthy church? Whether you are new to community groups or tired from years of challenging ministry, *Life-Giving Groups* is a fresh, practical invitation to life together in Christ.

Charting the Course: "How-To" Navigate the Legal Side of a Church Plant by Tim Beltz

Planting a church? It's time to plot the course toward legal validity.
Church planting is overwhelming enough before dealing with the legal and business regulations of founding a church. *Charting the Course* is for anyone, at any experience level to learn how to navigate the legal side of planting a church.

Redemptive Participation: A "How-To" Guide for Pastors in Culture by Mike Cosper

Our culture is confused. And so are we. It's not just you or them. It's all of us. But we can move past confusion and into a place of careful discernment. *Redemptive Participation* brings awareness to the shaping forces in our current culture and how to connect these dynamics with our teaching and practice.

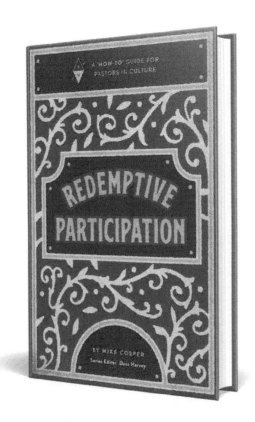

Filling Blank Spaces: "How-To" Work with Visual Artists in Your Church by Michael Winters

In the beginning, the earth was empty. Blank spaces were everywhere. *Filling Blank Spaces* addresses a topic that usually gets blank stares in the church world. But Winters is a seasoned veteran of arts ministry and has developed a premier arts and culture movement in the United States, without elaborate budgets or celebrity cameos. Instead, this guide gives a "How-To" approach to understanding visual art as for and from the local church, steering clear of both low-brow kitsch and obscure couture. If you are ready to start engaging a wider, and often under-reached, swath of your city, while awakening creative force within your local church, then this book is for you.

Before the Lord, Before the Church: "How-To" Plan a Child Dedication Service by Jared Kennedy with Megan Kennedy

Is child dedication just a sentimental moment to celebrate family with "oohs and ahhs" over the babies? Or is it a solemn moment before God and a covenanting one before the local church? Kennedy explains a philosophy of child dedication with poignant "How-To" plan for living out a powerful witness to Christ for one another and before the watching world. Whether you are rescuing various forms of child dedication from sentimentalism or perhaps sacrament, this book will guide you to faithful and fruitful ministry honoring God for the gift of children while blessing your church.

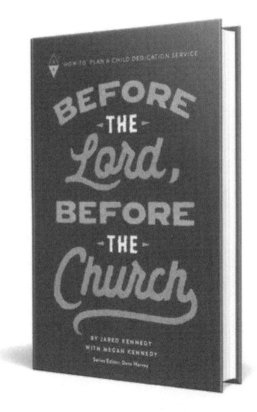

Sabbaticals: "How-To" Take a Break from Ministry before Ministry Breaks You by Rusty McKie

Are you tired and worn out from ministry? Isn't Jesus' burden supposed to be light? In the pressure-producing machine of our chaotic world, Jesus' words of rest don't often touch our lives. As ministry leaders, we know a lot about biblical rest, yet we don't often experience it. The ancient practice of sabbath provides ample wisdom on how to enter into rest in Christ. *Sabbaticals* is a guide showing us how to implement Sabbath principles into a sabbatical as well as into the ebb and flow of our entire lives.

Leaders through Relationship: "How-To" Develop Leaders in the Local Church by Kevin Galloway

The church needs more godly leaders. But where do they come from? Some people read leadership books in a season of rest and health. But if we're honest, most often we read leadership books when we're frazzled, when we see the problems around us but not the solutions. If you're feeling the leadership strain in your church, let Kevin Galloway show you a way forward, the way of Jesus, the way of personally investing in leaders who then invest in other leaders—because making an intentional plan to encourage and train leaders, is not a luxury; it's mission critical, for your health and the health of your church.

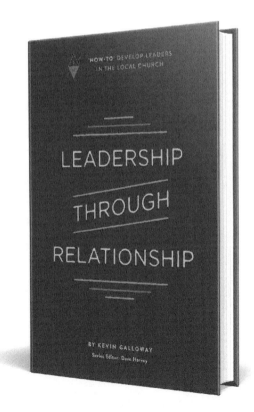

Raising the Dust: "How-To" Equip Deacons to Serve the Church by Gregg Allison & Ryan Welsh (forthcoming)

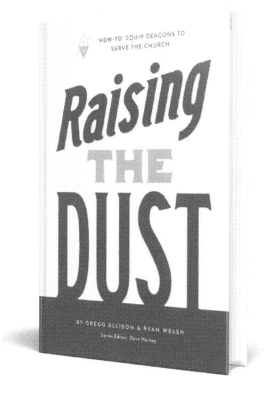

Made in the
USA
Columbia, SC

82359588R00074